# The Enlisted Leader

A Non-Commissioned Officer's Guide to Leading Airmen & Guardians in the 2020s

Daryl J. Hogan Jr.

DARYL J. HOGAN JR.

Copyright © 2021 Daryl J. Hogan Jr.
All rights reserved.
ISBN: 9798465354653
ISBN-13

## Books by Daryl J. Hogan Jr.

It's More Than a Job: Life and Leadership through the Eyes of a First Sergeant

Life of a Command Chief: Lessons Learned During My First 12 Months on the Job

## DISCLAIMER

The views and opinions in this book are solely those of the author and do not reflect official sanctioning or endorsement by the Department of Defense or any branch of the United States military.

No part of this book may be reproduced in any form without permission in writing from the publisher, except by a reviewer, who may quote brief passages in a review.

## DEDICATION

I dedicate this book to my stepdad, Vincent, who has been an outstanding father, role model and positive difference-maker in my life.

# CONTENTS

|   | | |
|---|---|---|
| | Preface | Page 1 |
| 1 | Transformational Followership | Page 3 |
| 2 | Leading with Purpose & Passion | Page 13 |
| 3 | Failing Forward | Page 21 |
| 4 | Counseling, Mentoring & Sponsoring | Page 27 |
| 5 | Social Media Behavior | Page 33 |
| 6 | A Hard Look at Diversity & Inclusion | Page 37 |
| 7 | Your Chief Didn't Walk on Water | Page 45 |
| 8 | Juggling Family Life & Work Life | Page 51 |
| 9 | W.I.N. Philosophy | Page 57 |
| 10 | Q&A with Air and Space Chiefs! | Page 63 |
| 11 | Today's Threat, Tomorrow's War | Page 87 |
| 12 | The Last Best Hope for America | Page 97 |
| | Bibliography | Page 99 |
| | Acknowledgments | Page 105 |
| | About the Author | Page 107 |

DARYL J. HOGAN JR.

# PREFACE

The purpose of this book is to mentor, educate and spark curiosity among non-commissioned officers (NCOs) that will encourage them to pursue a deeper study into all of the topics addressed. The information is presented in a conversational tone as opposed to what may be found in a scholarly journal to enhance its readability and practical application. There are countless books on leadership effectiveness, but the author has written this one specifically with NCOs in mind who serve in the US Air Force and US Space Force.

The role of an NCO is unlike any other. There are many similarities between leading employees in the private sector and leading service members who have taken an oath to defend the United States of America. There are also countless differences. NCOs have the unique challenge of motivating and inspiring young men and women who have promised to sacrifice their lives, if necessary, for the good of their units and their country.

If you are looking for a watered-down, politically correct book that gives you all of the company answers on leadership, this is not the one. The author pulls no punches while directly addressing often controversial topics such as toxic followership, social media behavior, and parts of American history that have led to recent diversity and inclusion discussions. Much of the mentorship and guidance presented is beneficial to NCOs serving in all branches of the US military and leaders working in the private industry. Still, unapologetically, this book is targeted toward military supervisors.

This is not a 10-step "how-to" guide. What you will find between these pages is the passionate mentorship of several chief master sergeants directed at the phenomenal NCOs who serve our nation in the profession of arms from across the globe. It is brief, blunt, and written for leaders on the go who do not have time to navigate hundreds of pages while tackling their daily tasks. This is the book that every NCO should read! Readers should approach each chapter with an open mind, a teachable spirit, and a willingness to research the topics discussed in an effort to gain greater knowledge and a better understanding that will enhance their leadership effectiveness.

# CHAPTER 1
## Transformational Followership

Newsflash! Your favorite Chief Master Sergeant of the Air Force (CMSAF) takes or used to take orders and direction from the Secretary of the Air Force (SECAF) and the Chief of Staff of the Air Force (CSAF). The Chief Master Sergeant of the Space Force (CMSSF) walks in alignment with the Chief of Space Operations (CSO). Every command chief you have ever known or seen follows the orders of their wing commander. Regardless of enlisted rank, we are all followers in one respect or another. There is no reason to be ashamed of that. Followers serve in many of the highest offices of our nation. Even the Joint Chiefs of Staff follow orders and directions from the President of the United States and the Secretary of Defense. Hopefully, that puts followership in perspective for you. If you are not a "transformational follower," which I will describe later in this chapter, you should not plan on ever holding a senior leadership position.

**Attitude:** As a young Airman, I often heard non-commissioned officers (NCOs) say, "Look sharp because your uniform is the first thing that people see, and first impressions are lasting impressions." Those were during the days when we wore battle dress uniforms (BDUs) and spit-shined our black boots. If you wore a nicely ironed uniform with shiny boots, you would have the opportunity to be highlighted to distinguished visitors at your work centers. This opinion may be an over-generalization, but a person's performance was not the great discriminator; appearance was. I knew several sharp-looking Airmen who were less than stellar at their jobs.

What I learned over time was that attitude is the first thing that people see or experience when they make contact with you. How do you greet a Chief when she walks into the building or a commander when he stops to ask a question? What do you say about your squadron when a new Airman arrives from technical training or a Guardian PCSes in (permanent change of station)? Your attitude dictates your responses and speaks to the type of NCO that you are. And if you have the right attitude, your uniform will, in turn, look sharp because you take pride in your appearance, unless you are getting your hands and uniform dirty. When your hands are dirty from work, your focus is where it should be, on the mission. As maintainers and civil engineers know, the task is often a messy job. **\*Note\*** Looking sharp while knee-deep in aircraft parts does not require an ironed uniform and shiny boots. Few things are sharper than a professional with laser-focus on the task at hand.

I have heard it said that "your attitude determines your altitude." There is quite a bit of truth in that statement. Our attitudes are a reflection of our worldviews, our determination, and our resiliency. How does one overcome poverty, an unhealthy upbringing, an abusive relationship, and many other unwanted events if not by attitude? How do special operators traverse seemingly impossible physical and mental challenges if not with attitude or precisely a "can-do" attitude?

To bring this point home, every NCO should understand that one of the few things they can control in their life is their attitude, and attitude is a critical component of transformational followership. Is a person a leader if they do not have followers? Is it possible to be an exceptional leader with consistently lackadaisical followers? I would argue that the answer is "No" to both of those questions. Great followers can make even average leaders look good. Transformational followers enhance the scope of each task in which they direct their efforts.

When CSAF C.Q. Brown penned his historic 8-page strategic approach entitled *Accelerate Change or Lose* and outlined his priorities of focusing on Airmen, addressing bureaucracy, competition, and design implementation, CMSAF JoAnne Bass set out to ensure that every enlisted Airman in the US Air Force enterprise knew and understood the CSAF's direction. From military installation to military installation and from country to country, the CMSAF drew the bridge between what Airmen did at the tactical level and what the Department of the Air Force was doing at the strategic level to ensure our nation's security. That is the epitome of strategic followership. Building those bridges and following the marching orders of our superiors takes a dedicated and productive attitude.

NCOs who operate with the right attitude in the profession of arms do not necessarily always agree with their superiors or fully understand the reasoning behind every decision. Those NCOs know that they have a vital role in the organization and that others depend on their ability and willingness to get the job done. They also have faith that what they do as a service is necessary to defend our nation and continue our American way of life.

**Work Ethic:** Dr. Martin Luther King Jr. once stated,
> "If a man is called to be a street sweeper, he should sweep streets even as Michelangelo painted, or Beethoven composed music, or Shakespeare wrote poetry. He should sweep streets so well that all the hosts of heaven and

earth will pause to say, here lived a great street sweeper who did his job well."[1]

Whether you work in personnel or cyber security, fire and emergency services, finance, intelligence, or security forces, your work ethic should be your calling card. If you hail from a hard-working family, continue that legacy. If you were brought up in an environment where hard work was scoffed at, rewrite the narrative. Do your best to remove the phrase, "That's not my job," from your vocabulary when going above and beyond your regular duties enhances your organization's ability to get the mission accomplished, even if it means taking out the trash.

Part of transformational followership is seeing what needs to be done and doing it if it falls within the scope of your abilities. Great followers most often do not wait to be told what to do. They either identify what needs to be done and do it or ask what needs to be done and do it. And when they do what needs to be done, they do it so that they would be proud to have their work highlighted to the base populace at large, even if it is just taking out the trash; for no one wants to approach a dumpster with garbage spread around the outside of it. So, suppose we should be meticulous with even minor tasks. How much more should we work hard at protecting our installation, guarding nuclear weapons, ensuring personnel records are appropriately handled, following technical orders, etc.?

Transformational followers have exemplary work ethics that make their entire organization look good. And few things are more satisfying than knowing that you invested your heart and soul into a hard day's work. Think about this: when someone in public sees you in uniform and says,

"Thank you for your service," they are assuming that you carry on the legacy of hard work that was characterized by those who served before us.

**Job Proficiency:** Few things in your military career are more important than your job proficiency--very few things. We all join the Air Force and Space Force for different reasons (ex: education, travel, family history of service, patriotism, etc.). But we all have the same expectations levied upon us following our graduation from Basic Military Training, and that is to become proficient in our given specialty.

Transformational followers serving as sergeants, staff sergeants, and technical sergeants must maintain and continue to develop a level of proficiency that gets the job done promptly and improves or reengineers how the job is done. Junior enlisted Airmen learn and attempt to master their basic skills and duties. Non-commissioned officers should be scanning their professional industries (ex: firefighters, medical service personnel, electricians) to identify best practices, alternative methods, and evolving technologies that can be adopted in their work centers.

The most basic expectation of all service members is to follow legal orders and perform their jobs exceptionally well to meet the strategic goals of the Department of Defense, which ensures America's security and furthers its interests across the globe. The scope of responsibility of transformational followers to meet this end should not be understated. The impact of one Defender who allows an unauthorized entry on the installation, one loadmaster who doesn't properly secure the cargo on a C-130, or one intelligence analyst who removes top secret information from a secure facility can be catastrophic. Above all else, America needs service members to do their jobs well.

**Professional Development:** Developing professionals is the responsibility of the institution and the individual. Institutionally, Airmen and Guardians may attend Professional Military Education (PME) academies, complete career development courses (CDCs), and participate in on-the-job training (OJT). Individually, enlisted service members are expected to take personal initiative to further their development.

Unfortunately, enlisted members aren't provided the same institutional opportunities as commissioned officers are to gain college degrees. That is unfortunate because those same enlisted members operate and maintain multi-million dollar platforms that are much more technologically advanced than they were 20 or 30 years ago. But do not fret. There are plenty of programs and opportunities for enlisted members who have the initiative to obtain college degrees through a myriad of institutions that have partnered with the Air Force. And I would be remiss not to mention each enlisted Airman's ability to obtain a Community College of the Air Force (CCAF) associate degree accredited through the Southern Association of Colleges and Schools.

Transformational followers do not sit back, complain, and lament the opportunities they think they should have. They instead recognize that their options are probably twice as numerous as the generations preceding them. They take advantage of what is currently available, and they find ways to create new opportunities for themselves and their teammates. NCOs must realize that their professional development is critical to evolving into transformational and strategic followers.

**Private Organizations:** "Private orgs," or "POs" for short, should be near and dear to every NCOs heart. Organizations such as the Rising 6 Club, the 5/6 Club, and the Air Force Sergeants Association provide opportunities for NCOs to network with their peers in different career fields while also contributing to significant events on nearly every Air Force and Space Force base. Participation is key to celebrating heritage, promoting military culture, and recognizing the contributions of service members.

Transformational followers, whenever possible, participate in POs because they understand the benefits and the historical legacy that comes with membership in these organizations. They also know that the collective force of transformational followers from various career specialties is the recipe for enhancing professional growth and making a positive difference in the local community through volunteerism and active citizenship.

**Toxic Followership:** This topic is certainly not addressed enough, if at all, in military circles. We have all heard of toxic leadership, and many of us have worked with or for toxic leaders. What we tend to turn a cold shoulder to is the one entity that degrades the efforts and image of countless organizations: toxic followers. The polar opposite of a transformational follower is a toxic follower.

Nearly every organization has them, and we all know who they are. Toxic followers find the negatives in every situation. If there is not a negative to be found, they will create one. Some feel entitled, a few are disgruntled, some are driven by jealousy, and others find satisfaction in disrupting any effort they did not initiate. So how do we identify them?

Toxic followers are the individuals who consistently complain about the way things are, even when things are good. They make off-colored jokes in the work center, often targeted at race, gender, sexual orientation, ethnicity, politics, or religion. They undermine the chain of command, constantly take shortcuts, even when unsafe, and disparage the very organization in which they voluntarily enlisted. These "professional cancers" take great efforts to find like-minded individuals or proselytize others into their warped way of thinking. Beware, young, and impressionable Airmen and Guardians may be their targeted population. These cowards also hide behind aliases on social media while taking virtual jabs at senior leaders, new policies, and strategic efforts. They plant seeds of doubt and spread misinformation. The actions of toxic followers can be more damaging than enemy forces because toxic followers destroy the fabric of organizations from the inside out.

Let us not be confused. I am in no way saying that complaining, wanting things to improve, or voicing one's opinion that is counter to the directions of senior leaders is toxic. What is being addressed here are individuals whose divisive words and actions consistently damage organizations or the perspectives of coworkers and teammates through efforts that provide no viable solutions. Do not be a toxic follower!

**Transformational Followership:** Having read this chapter, you should understand what a transformational follower is. Every NCO should strive to epitomize the attributes of a transformational follower. Transformational followers are difference-makers who improve teams through their unwavering commitment, enhance the output and productivity of organizations, carry out the legal orders of their superiors, strengthen national and strategic efforts, and improve themselves in ways that will enhance their military squadrons, deltas, wings, and headquarters staffs.

It can easily be argued that transformational followers are more important to many organizations than the average leader. Why? Transformational followers can serve in whatever capacity their work centers request, much like star athletes who are versatile and able to play multiple positions as needed. They are highly effective in their current roles. They maintain proficiency in jobs held by lower-ranking teammates, and they seek out a working knowledge of the duties performed by their peers. When needed, they step up into leadership positions to ensure that operations resume just as they would if their boss was at work.

Commanders do not have to look outside of their units to fill staffing gaps and interim vacancies when they have transformational followers on the team. The staff sergeant is ready to fill in when the technical sergeant takes a vacation, and the technical sergeant is more than prepared for added responsibilities when the master sergeant deploys for seven months. That readiness results from the time that NCOs spend learning the duties of the NCO or senior NCO above them. As one of my former supervisors used to say, "You need to always be ready to step into the two positions over yours. If you're not, someone else will be, and you'll be taking orders from them." Do not misunderstand me. When your peers get opportunities to serve in higher capacities, ensure that you are first in line to support and celebrate them. When your time to advance comes, answer your call with humility, confidence, and competence. Stay ready!

[1] L. Friedman (2017). "10 Inspiring MLK Quotes on Leadership and Purpose." *Entrepreneur*.

DARYL J. HOGAN JR.

# CHAPTER 2
## Leading with Purpose & Passion

If you have matured and developed as a transformational follower, you can begin to enhance your growth and abilities as a leader in your organization. It is my belief that the best leaders lead with purpose and passion. Some are extroverted, and others are introverts, but they all lead with purpose and passion. Suppose a leader has not found her purpose. In that case, she is probably blindly leading her followers in a direction that does not maximize mission effectiveness. And suppose a leader is not leading with passion. He is perhaps guiding his subordinates in a way that does not capitalize on their capabilities.

**What is your professional purpose?** NCOs must understand their professional purpose to be maximally effective. Shift supervisors at Starbucks understand that their purpose is to manage shifts and enhance the experiences of baristas and customers while providing world-class coffee on behalf of the 110 billion-dollar company.[1] Operations managers at Amazon understand that their professional purpose is to supervise and support frontline managers as they strive to meet production goals for the 314 billion-dollar company.[2] The US Air Force and US Space Force do not have a net worth, per se, so what is the professional purpose of NCOs?

While the two military services may not have a net worth, they do have customers. Both the US Air Force and US Space Force provide a service to the nation in the form of national security, as well as to our country's allies and partners. This is largely made possible by our NCO corps that "deliver[s] the military's biggest asymmetric advantage."[3]

Service-members generally represent just one aspect of America's national instruments of power, captured in the acronym DIME (diplomacy, information, military, and economy). Still, it is the one aspect that can rain immediate death and destruction on enemy nations.

In short, the professional purpose of NCOs is to execute tactics and supervise other warriors who execute tactics that deliver the necessary effects required to ensure mission success during wartime, peacetime, and humanitarian operations. There are thousands of individual tasks within those NCO responsibilities, many dependent upon a service member's respective career field. An Airman might find himself leaping from a C-17 aircraft at high altitudes behind enemy lines or assisting a retired master sergeant with obtaining a new identification card at the military personnel building. A Guardian may be required to train new arrivals on tracking space debris while working in a sensitive compartmented information facility, or she could be forging future American warriors while serving as a military training instructor at Lackland Air Force Base in Texas.

Regardless of what job you are currently serving in, NCOs within the profession of arms can find their professional purpose in their respective service's mission statements. The mission of the US Air Force is "To fly, fight, and win…airpower anytime, anywhere."[4] That is the service that Airmen provide to their customers. That is the purpose and the promise of NCOs serving in the US Air Force. Those eight words should undergird everything that NCOs do, whether training junior enlisted Airmen, fixing aircraft, troubleshooting computers, directing air traffic, treating patients, calling in close air support, teaching professional military education, or preparing meals at the dining facility.

14

Understanding your purpose as an NCO is vital to finding success as a leader. And every leader should be aware of their strengths.

**Identify your strengths:** Are you an exceptional communicator or public speaker, a good listener or organizer? Maybe you are an empath or a team builder, a fitness guru, or an analytic. What do your coworkers call on you for? Have you mastered a particular aspect of your job? Do your supervisors and commanders rely on you for specific things that your peers do not seem to provide? If you are unsure, seriously consider getting feedback from your supervisors and subordinates. Sometimes our true talents are recognized by everyone except for us.

Consider this, on average, major league baseball pitchers throw game-time fastballs at approximately 91 miles per hour.[5] Hall of Famer Nolan Ryan is believed to have thrown a record-setting 108 miles per hour fastball.[6] Wow! If a high school or collegiate pitcher can throw consistently above 100 miles per hour, which is rare, there is a pretty good chance that he will be drafted in the first round. Indeed, if the only thing that a pitcher threw was fastballs, he would tire out reasonably quickly. The batters would eventually adapt to his one trick. But pitching is situational, so it is essential to have other skills in the repertoire. Even a pitcher who could throw amazingly fast would likely include a few curveballs and the occasional slider during his time on the mound. But, without a doubt, his position on the team is secured because of his fastball.

Leadership is also situational, and NCOs should be a "jack-of-all-trades," so to speak. Identifying, developing, and leveraging a specific strength or two can genuinely catapult a leader's career. More importantly, learning to leverage your strengths can pay dividends for the Airmen and Guardians you lead. For example: by taking advantage of opportunities to provide motivational speeches at graduations, promotion ceremonies, etc., I inspired Airmen and Guardians that I otherwise may not have communicated with while also creating an avenue that encouraged them to approach me for mentorship. Motivational speaking was just one tool in my bag (my 100-mph fastball). Still, I was able to leverage it to build relationships, get to know my teammates, and provide life and career counseling. While each NCO should identify their fastballs, they must also be honest and open-minded about their weaknesses.

**Identify your weaknesses:** It has been my experience that most leaders do not like to talk about or highlight their shortcomings. But, here is another newsflash: we all have them. The goal should be to work on and minimize them, but you cannot fix what you will not admit to. So, what are your weaknesses? If you do not know, here is another opportunity to get feedback from your supervisors and subordinates.

Do you have a short temper or short attention span? Do you typically judge a situation before getting all the facts or formulate responses without hearing out your Airmen? Is your worldview driven by the sole news channel that you watch, or do you generally make decisions based on preconceived notions that you grew up with? Do you know the names of immediate family members of the Guardian's that you supervise, or what motivates your subordinates to go above and beyond the call of duty? Are you willing to admit to and then work on minimizing your weaknesses? I hope that you are because doing so is absolutely vital to leading with purpose.

**What is your professional passion?** You will likely find your professional passion in the aspects of your job that you love the most. A firefighter may discover that her favorite days at work are when she gets to instruct classes for her shift. A vehicle mechanic may realize that he thoroughly enjoys the days when asked to conduct inspections and perform equipment inventory checks. An NCO working in the base gym may be partial towards organizing intramural sports seasons, and the section chief for a fabrication flight may enjoy creating metallic going-away gifts for departing squadron members.

Finding your professional passion is a great way to continue falling in love with your job. When that happens, performing your duties is a lot less like work and more like indulging yourself in a hobby. I cannot count the number of times I have seen an Airman drenched in sweat and covered in dirt and oil with the biggest and most satisfying smile on his face. When you are fully engaged in an aspect of your job that you love, it is disappointing when someone wakes you from your trance to tell you that the shift is over.

I know. I know. Someone reading this may be saying to themselves, "I have never felt like that at work." That is entirely understandable, and it is also possible that the person could be stressed out and task-saturated with every aspect of the job. But suppose there is something…anything that captures your amusement or piques your interest about your duties or opportunities to participate in other capacities on base. I encourage you to seize it. Whether it is within your primary responsibilities, secondary duties, or tertiary opportunities, grab it! An NCO that can find passion within her job is an NCO that is destined for greatness.

**How do you lead with purpose and passion?** To lead with purpose and passion, NCOs must be deliberate about their actions. They must also understand that the respect required to lead effectively must be renewed each day and with every engagement. Understanding where and how your duties fit your squadron's goals and where and how your squadron's plans fit into the installation commander's goals is a great starting point. You can then leverage that knowledge to the most tactical level to ensure wide-ranging compliance and mission accomplishment.

Mission accomplishment entails more than just showing up for work, doing a good job, and going home. I repeat, you must be deliberate with your actions. NCOs must share their knowledge with other Airmen and Guardians to foster buy-in, esprit de corps, and ownership among their followers. And NCOs should exude the type of excitement about the mission that they want to see in their subordinates. It is very easy to get excited about your job when you understand the "why" and your leaders come to work visibly passionate about what your team is putting its collective efforts towards.

NCOs must also be deliberate about taking the time to get to know their Airmen and Guardians. You have to understand what makes them tick; what motivates them. Some will be driven to go the extra mile at work by the potential for quarterly awards; others will simply require a "Good job" compliment. Some Guardians will put forth additional effort in their duties to become commissioned officers. In contrast, others are just happy to have a full-time job to support their loved ones. No two followers are the same. Many of your subordinates have stories of resilience and perseverance that are nothing short of amazing. Get to know their stories!

What every Airman and Guardian needs is an NCO who is an authentic leader. One who cares about their followers and values their opinions. Our service members need NCOs who understand and live out their professional purpose while passionately tackling everyday tasks. They need NCOs who are willing to invest their time in them, inspire them, and encourage them to reach and achieve beyond what they believe is possible.

NCOs must be mindful that there will usually be specific individuals with whom they quickly connect due to hometowns, favorite sports teams, similar hobbies, etc. But leaders should be careful to spend equivalent time with each of their subordinates. They must not fall victim to making decisions based on personal biases or unethical favoritism. They must also be aware of how each of their professional relationships is perceived by others.

Lastly, leaders who are geographically separated from their followers should make time to regularly engage with their teammates, even if it is only via telephone calls or virtual platforms. If an NCO is on a different shift than her Airman, she must be dedicated enough to come in earlier or stay at work later, from time to time, in an effort to build the professional bonds needed to effectively supervise. Leading with purpose and passion sounds like a lot because it is. But it is also one of the most rewarding things leaders will ever experience.

---

[1] H. Kabra (2021). "Starbucks Net Worth 2021." *MD Daily Record.*
[2] B. Zhang (2021). "How Much Is Amazon Worth." *Yahoo! Finance.*
[3] J. Garamone (2019). "Noncommissioned Officers Give Big Advantage to U.S. Military." *U.S. Dept of Defense.*
[4] J. Dewberry (2021). "Air Force unveils new mission statement." *U.S. Air Force.*

[5] T. Sawchik (2021). "In The Age Of Velocity, Should MLB Teams Be Placing More Emphasis On Command?" *Baseball America*.
[6] SI Staff (2013). "The 10 Most powerful pitchers in baseball history." *SI/MLB*.

# CHAPTER 3
## Failing Forward

Staff Sergeant, you do not have to be perfect. You just need to pursue excellence. Tech Sergeant, you do not have to have all of the answers. You just need to be willing to go and find them. Do not be afraid of making a mistake or getting knocked down. You should only fear the refusal to take calculated risks and the unwillingness to dust off your pants, get back up and try again. Failing is a part of the process. Michael Jordan, arguably the greatest professional basketball player of all-time once stated:

> "I've missed more than 9,000 shots in my career. I've lost almost 300 games. Twenty-six times I've been trusted to take the game-winning shot and missed. I've failed over and over and over again in my life. And that is why I succeed."[1]

Kobe Bean Bryant, my all-time favorite basketball player and creator of the philosophical mindset known as the "Mamba Mentality," had the following to say about work ethic and failure:

> "I can't relate to lazy people. We don't speak the same language. I don't understand you. I don't want to understand you... I have self-doubt. I have insecurity. I have fear of failure. I have nights when I show up at the arena and I'm like, 'My back hurts, my feet hurt, my knees hurt. I don't have it. I just want to chill.' We all have self-doubt. You don't deny it, but you also don't capitulate to it. You embrace it."[2]

I could not have expressed the reality of failure being a part of the growth process better than Jordan and Kobe. Although, I do expect NCOs to understand the difference between failing forward and failing backward. Air Jordan and the Black Mamba, as they are affectionately called, failed forward. They took the risks and chances necessary for their ultimate goals and the goals of their respective teams. They identified, confronted, and even embraced their shortfalls while making every effort to grow, develop and overcome their weaknesses. Through much trial and error, they were victorious. They failed forward.

While supervising, leading, and mentoring Airmen and Guardians, you will not always get it right. Your advice may be slightly off-target. Your decisions may be ill-informed. Your explanations may be confusing. Your logic may be faulty. But your intentions must always be pure. It is rarely talked about, but NCOs and their subordinates actually grow and develop together. While Airmen are learning how to be transformational followers, NCOs are learning how to be servant leaders. The NCOs need the Airmen in this process as much as the Airmen need the NCOs. They both make mistakes, figure out solutions and produce better results together. They fail forward.

Failing backward is what must be avoided. When the risks taken are unsafe, unethical, immoral, or illegal, we fail backward. When nuclear weapons are unintentionally flown over the US or nuclear missile fuses are accidentally shipped to another country… that is failing backward. When unnecessary risks are taken that result in another person's injury or death… that is failing backward. When an NCO refuses to admit and own up to his mistake or repeats mistakes without learning from them... that is failing backward. When a leader abandons his responsibility to supervise and double-check the work of his Airmen, causing a critical mission delay or breach of security... that is failing backward. We as service members must continue to fail forward and do our best to never fail backward.

In all honesty, as an NCO, I failed both backward and forward. It would be hypocritical of me to act as if I had not. Supervising is a journey, not a destination. I had a lot to learn as a young staff sergeant (SSgt) if I planned to supervise effectively. Let me share a couple of stories that will hopefully help you avoid a few silly mistakes that I made.

The transition from senior airman (SrA) to SSgt, in my opinion, is the hardest transition from one rank to another that an enlisted member will ever make. Senior airmen sit at the top of the junior enlisted tier and tend to have a solid social structure in place. They are the Airmen that the new troops look to for guidance, direction, and understanding. In a nutshell, senior airmen are very often the cool kids on the block. That was me. I was a jokester who knew how to be the life of the party, a self-appointed dormitory king. Life was good. I made jokes, and people laughed. I played "the dozens," and no one was offended. That is until I was promoted to SSgt.

Seemingly overnight, I transitioned from being one of the guys to a leader who supervised the guys. My previous social structure had shifted, but my attitude had not. I had gone from standing at the top of the junior enlisted tier to sitting at the bottom of the NCO tier, and the expectations for my conduct had changed. I was suddenly responsible for managing the careers of others, upholding the NCO charge, and separating myself from the shenanigans of the younger Airmen, but I did not.

I continued to hang out with my old crew, party, and routinely crack jokes at the expense of others...including one particular Airman I supervised. I did not recognize how my behavior and jokes were degrading the professional relationship that was supposed to exist between an NCO and his subordinate. Jokes are not as funny when they are coming from your supervisor. When that particular Airman found himself in challenging situations concerning his marital life and career development courses, he needed a mature, caring, and responsible NCO in his corner. I tried to be that for him, but I had already assumed the role of a careless jokester who was more concerned about inciting laughs than being a leader, laser-focused on guiding professionals. That Airman chose to turn to other NCOs on our team with whom he had greater professional trust. I failed backward as an NCO in that scenario, and I regretted not being a better leader. Our relationship, both personal and professional, was never the same.

A year or so later, I failed forward. Upon returning from deployment, I was informed that I was the supervisor for "Airman Dranker," who had arrived from technical training four months prior. He came with an Article 15 punishment for underage drinking that had resulted in a lost stripe. By all accounts, Airman Dranker had been a model Airman and an outstanding firefighter since he showed up. By all accounts, except for that of our fire chief. Shortly after I met Airman Dranker, I was directed to write his annual appraisal. The fire chief's expectations were evident, "Give him a referral report so that he can't reenlist." I disagreed, and I found a loophole that allowed me to rate the appraisal in such a way that Airman Dranker was, in fact, allowed to reenlist. He was an outstanding firefighter, after all, who had simply made a victimless, bad decision during training.

24

In alignment with the guidance from our civilian leaders within the firehouse, I waited for the fire chief to go on vacation before submitting the final draft of the appraisal. It worked, sort of. Airman Dranker continued his military career and continued to thrive as he progressed through the ranks. Unfortunately, upon the fire chief's return from vacation and discovery of my actions, he called for me to report to his office. Interestingly, I was on vacation. I had been advised to take a few days off, to not be around when the fire chief arrived. He directed his secretary to call me at home, and I could hear him yelling and cursing in the background. She whispered that I should not answer my phone if I saw the fire station's number on my Caller-ID, for at least a day until he cooled off.

Eventually, I had to report to work and face the fire chief. He was a big man from "the mean streets of Chicago," as he put it, and he threatened to slap my lips off if I rolled my eyes at him one more time. He was disgusted at my act of what he perceived to be disloyalty. Fortunately, I had not broken any rules or regulations. The appraisal did not require the fire chief's signature or endorsement. As an act of reprisal, he downgraded my decoration when the time came for me to be reassigned, although I had won multiple awards. What I did wrong was hide, temporarily, from facing a challenge and from speaking truth to power. I failed to make my argument for why Airman Dranker should be given a second chance. I failed to have a discussion with the fire chief, one professional to another, before signing the appraisal. I failed to stand boldly as an NCO should. It took guts to do what I did, but it was also arguably a less than courageous approach. I learned from that experience. I began to stand on my principles, and I am proud to report that Airman Dranker was eventually promoted to master sergeant. I failed forward. You, too, will fail. It is a part of life, but I hope that you can learn vicariously through the successes and failures of others. *Fail forward…*

---

[1] (n.d.) "Thoughts On The Business Of Life." *Forbes Quotes.*
[2] A. Ichimura (2020). Kobe Bryant, Basketball Icon and Venture Capitalist: 15 Quotes from Mamba on Success, Failure, and Work Ethic.: *Esquire.*

# CHAPTER 4
## Counseling, Mentoring, & Sponsoring

NCOs have three of the most critical supervisory responsibilities: counseling, mentoring, and sponsoring their subordinates. Enlisted leaders must be deliberate about the growth of their Airmen and Guardians with an understanding that laissez-faire approaches to career development and team building most often result in confusion, misunderstandings, and a failure to help manifest the true talent in their teammates. Serving as an NCO is a full-contact sport that requires direct engagement.

**Counseling:** There are three basic types of counseling that all NCOs should be well versed in: career counseling, personal counseling, and corrective counseling. Very often, a counseling session may include two or all three of the above types. Career counseling can be given in a formal or informal setting. In the Air Force and Space Force, we place a lot of onus on personal responsibility, and rightfully so. Each individual is ultimately responsible for their own growth, but an Airman does not know what he does not know. NCOs must take "extreme ownership" of the growth and development of their subordinates. That is often done through career counseling.

The primary purpose of career counseling is not to teach Airmen or Guardians how to get promoted. It is not about checking boxes, so to speak. The primary purpose of career counseling is to build elite technicians who enhance the team and accomplish the service's mission with excellence. These elite technicians consequently perform in a way that typically results in grade or position promotions.

Every professional team utilizes a playbook or tactical plan for winning. The military services are no different. Airmen and Guardians need to understand their "playbook" or career paths based on job specialties, assignment possibilities, developmental special duties, educational opportunities, training expectations, etc. NCOs have to help their followers connect the dots between where they are and where they can go professionally, and how to progress in their job knowledge and job proficiency. Leaders also have to help their teammates understand the "why" in their duties to develop intrinsic motivation and a sense of purpose. This is all done through career counseling.

Personal counseling is where NCOs can genuinely build their professional relationship currency. Military service provides a unique opportunity to be more involved in the lives of your teammates and subordinates than most jobs outside of the base perimeter allow. In rare cases, NCOs are even expected to be intrusive to a certain extent. This is especially true when supervising young (ex: 17 to 21-year-old) troops who may be experiencing peer pressure or struggles with alcohol, finances, relationships, independence, etc.

Intrusive, as used in this context, could simply mean random or scheduled "check-ins" with members new to military service. Unlike what you will find at private sector companies, Airmen and Guardians who are new employees often reside in on-base dormitories or military housing. Many may feel very uncomfortable detailing their struggles to adjust to the military lifestyle or to report infrastructure or facility issues that they are experiencing. When NCOs can put "eyes on" the challenges that their subordinates are having, they are more likely to resolve those issues, which results in a better quality of life for their young teammates. In turn, young troops can come to work and actually focus on the tasks at hand instead of worrying about issues at home.

Corrective counseling is probably the aspect of counseling that gives young NCOs the most anxiety. It is also arguably the most crucial branch of the counseling tree. Corrective counseling requires patience, attention to detail, objectivity, and emotional intelligence. It could be as simple as reminding a young maintainer to follow the appropriate technical order when he forgets to. It can also be as complicated as helping a good-hearted subordinate overcome 18 years of trauma to better internalize the Air Force's core values and practice effective conflict management techniques.

NCOs must remember and accept that they do not know it all or have all of the answers. They should utilize their knowledge, personal experiences, and local resources to advise their troops. They should also know when a situation surpasses their ability to help and requires local chain-of-command or external assistance.

When considering corrective counseling, especially of a disciplinary nature, NCOs should understand potential cultural and other factors that guide their subordinates' decisions. Is your A1C experiencing financial issues because he sends his paychecks home to his parents? Is your 18-year-old airman basic distracted at work because she is planning a wedding? Does your senior airman need special religious accommodations to feel an inclusive work environment? No two situations are ever the exact same but conducting a simple root-cause analysis to uncover the "why" can go a long way to helping your troops resolve their own issues instead of putting a disciplinary bandage on them. Who knows? You could be developing a future officer, first sergeant, or Chief Master Sergeant of the Air Force. At a minimum, your actions will have a lasting impact on the lives of other human beings who have raised their hands to serve their nation.

**Mentoring:** Any NCO can counsel just about any Airman or Guardian, but mentoring is a whole other ballgame. Mentorship is generally a long-term professional relationship between two parties that very often extends well beyond one person supervising the other. As a matter of fact, a mentor may not currently supervise and may not have ever supervised the mentee. Very often, young troops do not realize that they need a mentor and do not understand the value and career impact of having a mentor. I like to think of mentors as the guiding light in an otherwise foggy career.

Think about it. When it is foggy outside, it is challenging to see what is ahead on the road you are traveling on. Is there debris on the street that should be avoided? Should you slow down because a deer is preparing to jump out in front of you? Should you speed up because you are slowing down traffic? Now imagine a young Guardian's career is that road. The mentor is the fog light that helps him see ahead and make better decisions to get him from Point A in his career to Point B in one piece.

Mentors are masters of communication and informal discussions. They help Airmen talk through and think through minor and major decisions, many of which have repercussions for their lives and careers. Mentors help mentees consider the risks involved, weigh the pros and cons of decisions, build plans of action, and remember what is truly important before deciding on a course of action. Counselors care about the mission. Mentors care about the Airmen and Guardians accomplishing the mission.

The best NCOs are both counselors and mentors in the same way that the best NCOs are both great leaders and managers. I would be remiss if I did not mention that an NCO should not be upset if their subordinate has multiple mentors. As a matter of fact, Airmen and Guardians should be encouraged to have more than one mentor so that they can benefit from a broader range of knowledge, experience, and perspectives. "Mentor" is one of the best professional titles that an NCO could ever hope to achieve.

**Sponsoring:** Sponsoring is a topic that is rarely discussed outside of senior leadership circles but is vitally important at every level of supervision. You may supervise the absolute best Airmen in the squadron or group. Still, if no one is there to advocate for them, they may never get the recognition or opportunities that they truly deserve. A rare deployment was just announced, or a point of contact is needed for a high-profile base event. You supervise an individual who would absolutely flourish in either capacity. What should you do? Should you wait for a senior leader to inquire about your subordinate, or should you engage with your chain-of-command to let them know you have the right person for the job? I think you know the correct answer.

What are you saying about your Guardians when they are not around? What do you tell senior enlisted leaders and commanders about them? How will your squadron commander know that it was your Airman who re-engineered a process that saved the unit thousands of dollars or man-hours? When your squadron is looking for a new unit fitness monitor or the installation is searching for new victim advocates, and you have a subordinate who would genuinely benefit from the experience, do you lobby for them?

After focusing efforts on counseling and mentoring, do not forget to seal the deal with sponsorship when the opportunity arises. It can be challenging for senior leaders to narrow down the right person for a duty or task when the pool of candidates is full of outstanding performers. Your sponsorship and ability to highlight why your Guardian is the best fit for an opportunity and how the space delta will benefit from selecting her are critical components of serving as an NCO.

# CHAPTER 5
## Social Media Behavior

"Is it Bass or Bass?" If you were an Airman or Guardian tuned in to Facebook in late 2020, you probably remember this infamous question online, aimed at our senior enlisted leader, and the wide-ranging opinions that followed. Most of us old-timers never thought we would see the day when top military leaders would be "trolled" by enlisted service members. Our Air Force core values (Integrity First, Service before Self, Excellence in all We Do) are hammered into our brains from the moment we step foot into Basic Military Training. Common sense in engaging with senior military leaders in-person, in training, during high-profile visits, etc., is almost a given. What appears not to be a given is how to engage with senior military leaders in the cyber domain during the age of social media.

Are the core values required on social media? Is mutual respect needed on social media? Do military leaders forgo their rank or authority on social media platforms like Facebook, Twitter, and Instagram? What about activities on an individual's personal social media pages as opposed to on official pages? These are questions that need to be answered and legitimate discussions that NCOs must have with their subordinates, peers, and teammates. As my stepdad would say, "Common sense isn't so common."

I am just going to shoot it to you straight like a Chief talking to an NCO during an informal mentoring session at the dining facility during lunch. Foolishness and shenanigans on social media are a readiness issue. Fifteen minutes of fame is not worth disciplinary actions, degrading the chain-of-command, or becoming a divisive internal force for our military. Think about it. Think about the impact that one comment, post, or picture can have on your unit. Think about the second- and third-order effects resulting from one service member trying to get a laugh or "cool points" out of their buddies. Think about going into work, and instead of your co-workers being focused on the aircraft sorties that are scheduled for the day or the sensitive launch mission that will require everyone's laser-focused attention, all the Airmen are talking about the racially insensitive joke that their flight chief posted on Facebook or the derogatory comment about a specific political party that a superintendent made on Twitter. Think about the breakdown in trust that would occur.

Imagine being in the unit that works extremely hard at ensuring national security but gets highlighted because of the decision of one senior airman or technical sergeant who makes a viral video that undermines the mutual trust required to accomplish the wing's mission. Would you consider that to be simply a lapse in judgment that is easily forgivable? Is that the team you would want to be on? Did you join the Air Force or Space Force to serve with individuals who prioritize a laugh or a personal opinion over what is best for their team?

Newsflash! Whether you are operating on earth, in space, or in cyberspace, the core values are as relevant and expected today as they were at Lackland Air Force Base, Texas, when you graduated from Basic Military Training. That means there needs to be a significant level of "excellence" when service members communicate on social media. There also needs to be an astute awareness that many of the comments and opinions attached to posts that act to divide our personnel and efforts are written by individuals

34

who have either never served in the US military or who are affiliated with external nations and groups that would like to see American society implode. Interestingly, those cowardly individuals lie, disguise, or misrepresent themselves as service members.

A war of words fought on social media is a battle lost. As many people quip, "the internet is undefeated!" The internet is a place where the weak can seemingly become strong, cowards can display false courage, and enemies of America can present themselves as fellow US troops in the hopes that our military forces will be gullible enough to believe every headline and disparaging comment that they read. It is the responsibility of our NCOs to keep their battle formations informed of the dangers and deceptiveness that are lurking on social media so that our primary focus, when duty calls, is on putting warheads on foreheads and not on who-said-what online.

DARYL J. HOGAN JR.

# CHAPTER 6
## A Hard Look at Diversity & Inclusion

In the year 2020, a perfect storm emerged that set the stage to change the role of the NCO for the next decade. Many Americans found themselves "teleworking" or working from home amid a growing pandemic and international health crisis. At the same time, children and young adults attended school virtually on their computers. It seemed as if everyone's eyes were glued to televisions and computer screens as the winter months faded away and an infamous spring ushered in societal and social unrest.

Breonna Taylor, a 26-year old black woman, and emergency room technician, was fatally shot by at least eight bullets when police officers stormed her apartment while executing a "no-knock" search warrant on 13 March 2020, just minutes after midnight.[1] As the details of the incident unraveled, many groups within American society became enraged. Countless citizens were out of work and off from school, many rebelling against federal and state-sponsored restrictions on travel and gatherings, and countless upset over political strife. It was as if the entire country was standing still, fearful of contracting the COVID-19 virus. It was a recipe for disaster.

On 25 May 2020, disaster struck. George Floyd, a 46-year old black man, was killed during his arrest following a 9-1-1 call from a convenience store. Americans at home glued to their television, computer, and smartphone screens watched in horror and disbelief as the cellphone footage recorded by a witness replayed nearly 24-hours a day. The footage showed George Floyd pleading for mercy, calling out to his deceased mother, and gasping for air under a police officer's weight who was kneeling on his neck for approximately eight minutes or more. George Floyd died in that position as a voice from the on-looking crowd cried out, "He is a human being!"[2] Shortly after that, the streets of our nation erupted with protests, riots, and rage. Racial tensions were not just high; they had reached their peak.

"He is a human being!" Therein lies much of what has plagued our nation for hundreds of years. You and I did not create this problem. We inherited this problem, but it is ours to fix if we want a better future for our children. "He is a human being!" Those five words reverberate a not too long ago time in our beloved nation when Northern and Southern states agreed upon the "Three-Fifths Compromise" in 1787, which directed that three-fifths of the slave population would be counted for determining direct taxation and representation in the House of Representatives.[3]

To translate the meaning: slaves were considered property and the compromise "elevated" their national status from mere objects to three-fifths of what a free person was for political purposes that did not benefit the slaves. They were still not given the fundamental human rights that other Americans enjoyed. Well, what does this have to do with America's modern military and our NCOs? Our nation's past set the stage for tensions that eventually bled over into the military.

Consider the Civil War, which was primarily fought over the very issue of slavery. As it progressed, blacks were enlisted to take up arms. Confederate General Clement H. Stevens stated, "I do not want independence if it is to be won by the help of the Negro…The justification of slavery in the South is the inferiority of the Negro. If we make him a soldier we concede the whole question."[4] By March of 1865, the North was making considerable progress, and Confederate President Jefferson Davis eventually conceded to enlisting 300,000 slaves with a promise of freedom if the South won the war. The strategic change, of course, came too late for the Confederacy. By the end of the Civil War, approximately 179,000 black men had served in the Union Army and another 19,000 in the Navy.[5] This is a part of our military history.

Progress was on the way, but slowly and against much opposition. In 1877, Henry O. Flipper became the first African American West Point Graduate.[6] John Alexander became the second black West Point graduate 10 years after Flipper in 1887.[7] Charles Young became the last black graduate of the prestigious military academy in 1889 for the next 50 years.[8] It is a bit of an unthinkable condition considering blacks and other minorities graduate from our military academies every year in modern times.

Blacks, such as the famed Buffalo Soldiers,[9] served through the Punitive Expedition and well into World War I before being succeeded by heroic groups such as the Harlem Hellfighters infantrymen,[10] the Triple Nickels firefighting paratroopers,[11] and our beloved Tuskegee Airmen[12] who changed how Americans looked at black pilots during World War II. Segregation ruled the day during the world wars. Racial tensions ran high as African Americans were forced to serve in all-black units and most often could not use the same facilities as their white counterparts. During this time, the Navy became home to the "Golden Thirteen," the modern Navy's first black officers. They were a group of men who recorded the highest class scores in the Reserve Officer Training Corps history at the school they attended.[13]

Yet, they were relegated to menial duties and domestic posts. And let us not forget the "Six Triple Eight" (6888th Central Post Directory Battalion), a segregated unit of courageous black women who served under Major Charity Adams, one of the first African Americans to graduate from the Women's Army Corps training program.[14] This, too, is our history.

When the Vietnam War kicked off, black and white troops were often serving side by side. Still, they were not immune to the divisive policies, practices, and social explosions that plagued America during the Civil Rights era. Yet, progress was being made. In his 1995 biography, Retired General Colin Powell stated:

> "The Army was living the domestic ideal ahead of the rest of America. Beginning in the fifties, less discrimination, a truer merit system, and leveler playing fields existed inside the gates of our military posts than in any Southern city hall or Northern corporation. The Army, therefore, made it easier for me to love my country, with all its flaws, and to serve her with all my heart."[15]

In the Air Force, service members witnessed the first black Chief Master Sergeant of the Air Force, Thomas N. Barnes, serve in the highest enlisted position from October 1973 to July 1977.[16] He was the first of any CMSAF to do a tour length that long. By the time Operation DESERT STORM rolled around in January 1991, General Colin Powell served as the first black-American, first Reserve Officer Training Corps graduate, and the youngest officer to ever hold the nation's highest military post as Chairmen of the Joint Chiefs of Staff.[17] In 2004, Merryl Tengesdal cross-commissioned from the Navy to the Air Force, eventually becoming the first black woman to fly the mysterious U-2 "Dragon Lady" spy plane, a feat unattained by many of the best pilots who set out to do it.[18]

The accomplishments of black Americans in the military by the time the 2000s were ushered in were nothing short of amazing, especially considering the American journey of those of African descent whose forefathers and foremothers had suffered through the horrific Transatlantic Slave Trade and "Jim Crow" laws. Yet, in December 2020, a Racial Disparity Report released by the Department of the Air Force's Inspector General[19] revealed what many black service members were already aware of; there is still much work to be done regarding diversity and inclusion in the military. That work, in large part, falls squarely on the shoulders of the NCOs who lead and guide our Airmen and Guardians.

The Racial Disparity Report revealed that, among other things, enlisted black service members are 72% more likely than their white counterparts to receive punishment under the Uniformed Code of Military Justice; black service-members are more likely to be suspects in criminal cases, and twice as likely to be apprehended by Security Forces; black service members are underrepresented in operational career fields and overrepresented in support career fields, which can have negative promotion impacts; and black service-members are underrepresented in promotions to E5-E7.[20]

Following the Breonna Taylor and George Floyd incidents, Airmen and Guardians could no longer hide behind the security of our fenced installations. Many had to navigate through protests and riots to get home after work, and just about all were inundated with storylines about America exploding into a race war every time they turned on the television or logged into their social media accounts. It was tough to remain neutral and silent. Society was demanding that we all pick a side.

The once-taboo topic of race in the workplace became a central theme on every installation. Even CSAF General David Goldfein and CMSAF Kaleth Wright addressed the issues very publicly. The inbound CSAF, General C.Q. Brown, serving as the Pacific Air Forces Commander, recorded a very emotional video entitled "Here's what I'm thinking about"[21] that detailed many of the experiences he had persevered through while serving as a black Airman. His candidness captured the attention of everyone who saw it. As NCOs, we could no longer go to work and not address the elephant in the room: race relations.

Bases began to host "tough talks" and "crucial conversations," specifically on the subject of race relations and what our Airmen and Guardians were experiencing. As a command chief, I hosted the first of these conversations for my base. I talked with countless Airmen and Guardians about their concerns, my perspectives, and our way forward. I went from squadron to squadron, participating in Commander's Calls and enlisted forums and attending senior leader discussions on race resulting in tears, openness, and stronger relationships. As a vital part of an installation command team, I saw measures taken, and growth developed that left us all a little better. The point is, we recognized that a problem lay before us that we could not hide from. The health and wellness of our teammates and the security of America were at stake. If there was one undeniable thing, it was that racial tensions are a readiness issue.

NCOs have got to take this bull by the horns. Racial tension is like cancer. It may be unseen and unfelt by some, but if it is there and it goes untreated, it will spread and destroy the host. This does not mean that NCOs should come to work every day and discuss race. It simply means that you must be aware that there are tensions and injustices in society and that they may exist in your unit; that Airmen and Guardians are affected by what happens on and off-post regarding race relations; that you must exercise emotional intelligence when discussing these issues with your teammates (and lead from a position of neutral); that you must be aware of your own personal prejudices and biases and how others perceive you; that you should make every effort to treat your teammates fairly; that you must be willing to grow and evolve your perspectives when presented with new information; that tough talks are uncomfortable for many but necessary for all; and that allowing a culture to exist within your workplaces where Airmen and Guardians do not trust one another, or your leadership, is a danger to your unit's mission and our national security. Simply put, be the change our nation needs!

---

[1] C. Carrega, S. Ghebremedhin (2020). "Timeline: Inside the investigation of Breonna Taylor's killing and its aftermath." *ABC News*.
[2] B. O'Neal (2020). "George Floyd's mother was not there, but he used her as a sacred invocation." *National Geographic*.
[3] Editors of Encyclopedia Britannica (n.d.). "Three-fifths compromise." *Brittanica*.
[4] (n.d.). "Juneteenth: 'The Emancipation Proclamation – Freedom Realized and Delayed.'" *Prairie View A&M Unviersity*.
[5] (n.d.). "Black Soldiers in the U.S. Military During the Civil War." *National Archives*.
[6] (n.d.). "Lieutenant Henry Ossian Flipper." *Center of Military History*.
[7] A. Braimah (2014). ""John Hanks Alexander (1864-1894). *Black Past*.

[8] (n.d.). "Colonel Charles Young." *National Park Service.*
[9] History.com Editors (2021). "Buffalo Soldiers." *History.com.*
[10] B. Chappell (2021). "An All-Black Unit That Fought Germany And Racism In WWI Gets Congressional Gold Medal." NPR.
[11] (n.d.). "555th Parachute Infantry." *TripleNickle.com.*
[12] (n.d.). "The Tuskegee Airmen." *Tuskegee University.*
[13] (n.d.). "The Golden Thirteen." *Naval History and Heritage Command.*
[14] K. Fargey (2014). "6888th Central Postal Directory Battalion. *U.S. Army Center of Military History.*
[15] (n.d.). "Say It Plain, Say It Loud: A Century of Great African American Speeches." *American Radio Works.*
[16] M. Haynes (2012). "Thomas N. Barnes: First African-American CMSAF." *US Air Force.*
[17] (n.d.). "Colin Luther Powell." *Joint Chiefs of Staff.*
[18] (n.d.). *Merryltengesdal.com.*
[19, 20] The Inspector General Department of the Air Force (2020). "Report of Inquiry/Independent Racial Disparity Review."
[21] C.Q. Brown (2020). "Here's what I'm thinking about." *Pacific Air Forces.*

## CHAPTER 7
## Your Chief Didn't Walk on Water

It is interesting how many Airmen and Guardians think the individuals serving as chief master sergeants must have had a perfect career with no missteps. It is actually laughable and far from the truth for most of us. The road to "Chief" is often paved with mistakes, less than great decisions, and the occasional correction in the form of counseling and administrative warnings. I believe it is essential for chiefs to share some of those missteps and how we overcame some of the challenges we faced as young Airmen. Now, for the record, I am not saying that I did any of the things that follow, but let's just say that I know a guy. It is strictly a coincidence that he happens to look just like me!

When I joined the Air Force... I mean, I know a guy who joined the Air Force with a world of potential but did not yet possess effective conflict resolution skills. He also did not recognize the bright future that lay ahead, or he would have made much better decisions early on. He did not take criticism well, and based on the societal culture where he grew up, he viewed verbal challenges, underhanded comments, and condescending remarks as an invitation for a physical altercation.

Needless to say, this young man had a few physical altercations between the ages of 18 and 20 while serving on active duty. One particular incident never crossed the threshold of yelling and screaming. Still, the recipient was an NCO, and the young Airman involved subsequently received a rating markdown on his annual evaluation. Yes, a blatant injustice had been committed against this Airman, but confronting an NCO in a hostile manner was the wrong way to address the issue. If it were not for a third party who stepped in to resolve the confrontation, that Airman might have lost his career just a couple of years after it began.

One of the things that the young Airman experienced almost immediately after arriving at his first duty assignment was a culture of drinking alcohol. Every off-duty shift gathering and every get-together in the dormitories involved alcohol. As if drinking and underage drinking were not enough, being part of the in-crowd meant occasionally drinking to excess, resulting in uncharacteristic behaviors and very brutal mornings. Luckily, it did not take too many hangovers to realize that one wrong decision while intoxicated could lead to a lifetime of dealing with the consequences. Unfortunately, a few of his peers realized that reality one or two drinks too late.

Other phenomenon that the young Airman experienced and witnessed during his initial years of service was bad relationships and a poor choice of friends. Not everyone serving on active duty is a rock star. And as human nature would have it, Airmen naturally gravitate towards people who have similar interests or come from similar places when they find themselves in new and foreign environments. That is not bad unless it is bad. What the Airman witnessed were certain young men and women who not only gravitated toward others with less than productive past lives, but who took the opportunity to polarize and exaggerate their pre-military social statuses to impress their friends. The Airman sometimes marveled, from a distance, at how these individuals not only recreated who they genuinely were, but also recreated who they used to be. It was the mid-90s version of building a false persona online; only, it was done in-person among strangers who could not validate or discredit their stories.

I generally steered... I mean, the Airman himself generally steered clear of those posers. Still, he failed to avoid the dreaded relationship blunders plaguing many youngsters with money in their pockets. It is amazing how money and a steady job make a person more attractive. Suppose that person has an actual career, and a dangerous or cool one at that. In that case, he or she will need repellant to keep the prospective boyfriends or girlfriends away. The Airman in this story made very poor relationship decisions that led to heartache, financial disasters, estranged children, and an eventual divorce. Luckily, his mistakes were made early in his career. He had a sound support system, mentors, and enough friends who believed in him to finally emerge as a mature human being, manifesting his true gifts.

The point is that none of us is perfect, not even chiefs. It took years of self-reflection for me... I mean, that Airman to realize his potential, surround himself with like-minded individuals who wanted to achieve great things in life, and stop playing the victim role for his shortcomings. He stopped making excuses and started accepting the part of the victor over his challenges instead of being a victim of societal stereotypes. But the Airman did not do it alone. He had great friends and supervisors like SSgt William Spears, SSgt Willie Wardy, and TSgt Gary Rucks, who guided him along the way.

Given the details presented in this story without knowing the outcomes, what would you as an NCO have done about this young Airman? Would you have written him off or given up on him? Would you have sought to understand his "why" while recognizing his potential and helping him forge a path to success? Chances are, this young Airman, or someone like him, is serving under your leadership right now. What will you do about it?

By now, you may be saying, "Yeah, Chief...but did you make any mistakes as an NCO?" I certainly did; too many to count. I was a lot more polished as an NCO than I was as a junior enlisted Airman, but I was not perfect (see Chapter 3). I can remember being one of many recipients of an email from another NCO while stationed overseas. The email was inappropriate, to say the least. It was the type of email that should not be sent over government computers. Like a good NCO, I did not forward it. Like a passive NCO, I did not address it. Eventually, the email was sent to someone who did report it to their chain of command, and everyone who had received it was called in and questioned. I was asked why I failed to report the situation or confront the NCO who initially sent the email during my questioning. I knew that my "lack of action" was wrong, but I also figured that I was no worse than anyone else who had received it. That is when I was informed that I was selected as the fire department's Firefighter-of-the-Year and asked if I thought I deserved it, given the circumstances. The notification and question cut me like a knife. I saw the disappointment in the eyes of my superiors. I realized how badly I had failed.

A few years later, while serving as a technical training instructor, I was quickly promoted to teach in our advanced courses. I had progressed from training Airmen who had recently graduated from Basic Military Training to educating seasoned firefighters who were serving around the globe. We had a hard-working team of instructors, and things were going well. So, when a new teammate did not appear to be pulling his weight, I promptly confronted him. My peers and

I expected more from someone who had served for more than 20 years, and we felt as if this one individual was causing more work for the rest of us. After multiple attempts to address the problem directly, I resorted to very loud verbal jabs that were well beneath the standards of firefighter instructors.

I put my supervisor in a very challenging position. He had to address my actions and bring harmony back to our otherwise high-performing team. Many senior NCOs would have responded with administrative measures that have a lasting impact on an individual's career. That is the easy way out. My supervisor considered my usual behavior, performance, and attitude, realized that this random day was an outlier, and decided to have a heart-to-heart with me that changed my career trajectory. Two years later, instead of leaving that assignment with derogatory paperwork, I left with an unexpected promotion to master sergeant and my first-ever installation annual award win. I did not walk on water, but I certainly had a support system that helped me stay afloat.

-------

*I would be remiss if I did not mention the true source of my resilience and awakening. I have heard that if you want to know how a thing operates, consult with its creator or the owner's manual. While serving at my first duty station in 1996, I ran across a little burgundy book in the dormitory dayroom. It was called The Teen's Topical Bible, and it presented scriptures under subtitles such as "What to do when you are angry" and "How to overcome peer pressure."

49

At 18 years of age, I could not have found that little jewel at a better time. Studying that little book began the renewal process of my heart and mind. In 1998, while attending a local bazaar at my second duty assignment in Northern Japan, I became fixated on a New Living Translation Bible. But when I looked at the price, I began to walk away. A stranger who I had never seen before and whom I cannot recall seeing again stopped me and said, "You should buy that one. It is really good." So, with hesitation, I bought it. It turned out to be a study bible written in plain English with commentaries that I could understand. Over time, it became the most significant contributor to my spiritual education. I still have both books today, more than 20 years later. And although they are falling apart, they helped me stay together, grow in faith and connect with God in a very personal way through the years. Focusing on our Creator instead of on my problems is how I transformed my mind and became an overcomer.*

# CHAPTER 8
## Juggling Family Life & Work Life

I have heard this said more times than I can count at retirement ceremonies: "I wish I would've spent more time with my family." Interestingly, I have never heard veterans say that they wish they would have spent more time at work. There seems to be a belief that serving on active duty means that our families have to suffer. While it is true that certain sacrifices will most likely have to be made, it is also true that the military experience should be one of the most exciting times in the lives of military families. That experience weighs heavily on the shoulders of the individual service member and their willingness to include their families into their bigger Air Force and Space Force family.

Spouses are too often uninformed, and that can have a very negative effect on military families. In my experience, they are uninformed because their beloved service members refuse to be transparent about services, support, events, and activities available for them and their children. Junior enlisted Airmen and NCOs often attempt to keep their work lives and family lives separate instead of blending them in a way that honors their families by making them an intricate part of the military experience. That is unfortunate for several reasons.

Airmen and Guardians should include their families in the broader military family because service members arrive at a duty station and receive an instant network of coworkers, friends, and channels for information. Conversely, their spouses arrive and usually do not know anyone, nor where to go for information about the unit or base activities and support for issues they may be having. For example, a new staff sergeant can go to work, integrate and get relief from stresses experienced at home. His spouse is in a foreign place trying to figure out how to make a house a home while seemingly isolated from the support of family and friends.

The military provides information on all the support available. Most likely, the staff sergeant's chain of command regularly sends emails about resources that families should take advantage of. Still, the message never gets to the staff sergeant's spouse. During his in-processing briefing, the first sergeant personally tells the staff sergeant about the squadron's phenomenal Key Spouse Program because it instantly integrates spouses into the unit's broader family and creates information flow among spouses. Yet, the staff sergeant chooses to not share the information with his loved one.

Too often, an NCO's chain of command does not meet his spouse and children until that NCO begins to fail at juggling family life and work life and bad decisions start to manifest. Even when poor choices do not result from mounting stress, NCOs must realize that isolating their families from information, resources, and the ability to grow a network of friends can make an otherwise great military assignment a dreadful experience. NCOs should also realize that several of their very own Airmen or Guardians may be doing that same thing: isolating their families.

Think about this, when it comes to working, the military will provide you with months of technical training, years of career development courses, computer-based training, on-the-job training, technical orders, supervisors, manuals, Air Force Instructions, upgrade training, and even a path to obtain your Community College of the Air Force degree. Everything mentioned above is directly related to your chosen profession. It is why you wear your uniform, and it is why you are so great at your jobs. Unfortunately, the same amount of training, manuals, and programs are not available on how to be a good husband, wife, or parent, and that is what so many of our otherwise outstanding junior enlisted Airmen and NCOs struggle with. It is why so many retirees say, "I wish I would've spent more time with my family." It is why so many of our best warriors make poor relationship decisions, have failed marriages, and finish their careers regretting the lack of time spent with their kids.

Newsflash: it does not have to be that way. There may not be the same amount of training and education available for being a good spouse and parent as there are for being a sound technician, but there is quite a bit available that many of our warriors do not take advantage of.

The Airman & Family Readiness Center (A&FRC), located on most bases, has a plethora of resources, information, and events for military families. NCOs should ensure that the A&FRC where they are stationed becomes a significant part of the military experience for their families. The local installation Youth Center often hosts youth sporting leagues, family cooking classes, etc., for military families. Other opportunities such as "Give Parents a Break" and "Parents Night Out" are also often offered to help spouses reconnect or take a breather from the hustle and bustle of daily life. These opportunities apply to single parents as well. Those programs cannot help you if you do not inquire about them or utilize them.

When struggling with adjusting to a new location, deployments, and/or work schedules, there are countless resources available for service members and their families, including the local chaplains, Military One Source, and local Military & Family Life Counselors, all at no cost to the military families. Service members do not have to be present when their loved ones utilize these services.

Lastly, I will address the Air Force's second core value, "Service before Self." Many NCOs misconstrue those three words to mean "Military First, Family Last." That is not at all the case or the intent. Putting your service before yourself means putting what is best for your team, unit, wing, Air Force, and country before your own personal desires. It means you will work odd or offset hours when needed, and you will deploy to foreign lands when necessary. It speaks to the fact that we will sometimes sacrifice our short-term personal goals to place greater focus on our service's long-term mission. As many of you already know, your duties will periodically result in you missing birthdays, holidays, anniversaries, recitals, your children's sporting events, etc., some of you more than others.

Your neighbor, an NCO of equal rank in another squadron, may be regularly available to attend parent-teacher nights while you generally miss out on them due to your job. Your spouse may notice that she is always the lone parent in your family at your kids' events. At the same time, it appears that other families have both mom and dad attending the same events with their kids. I will not sugarcoat it. Those can be challenging moments to bear. As the saying goes, "We serve and our families sacrifice." That is why it is so essential for NCOs (and all service members) to be deliberate about the time that they do spend with their families. Consider instituting family game nights, eating together at the dinner table instead of in separate rooms, and taking a few moments before entering your house to mentally adjust from being Sergeant (fill in your name) to being mom, dad, husband, or wife.

NCOs should also take the time to discuss work (when appropriate) with their families to better explain what challenges lay ahead and help them feel like an essential part of what their loved ones do for our nation. I cannot count the number of times I have asked my son's teenage friends what their mom or dad do in the Air Force, and they had no clue. I would later discover that they were an aircraft maintainer, a financial technician, or an electrician. I always found it sad that so many NCOs did not deem it necessary to discuss their careers with their kids. Maybe it is because even when they were home, they were absent. Think about that for a moment. Honestly, my wife had to remind me on more than one occasion to be present when I was home. It is very easy to be physically in your house after a long day's work but to be mentally still at work, or still deployed, or still in training. NCOs, when you are at work, be 100% at work. When you are home, be 100% at home. Do not give your family bits and pieces of you. Do not give them leftovers. Give them all of you, the best of you--the main dish. Make your personal core values, "Transparency First; Family before Self; Excellence in Marriage & Parenthood!"

# CHAPTER 9
## W.I.N. Philosophy

One of the ways that I articulate my professional perspective on leadership is through what I call the W.I.N. Philosophy. W.I.N. is an acronym for self-worth, emotional intelligence, and necessary to the mission. It was developed as a leadership solution to the emotional and mental anguish I witnessed in many Airmen. By exercising the W.I.N. Philosophy, we can all be better and more engaged leaders.

**Self-WORTH:** Airmen and Guardians come from every walk of life, and most join the military to be a part of a purpose that is bigger than themselves. While some come from very affluent backgrounds, others began their lives in very humble, and in some cases, impoverished settings. Whether previously fed with a silver or plastic spoon, Basic Military Training and technical schools are the great equalizers that unite our service members for a collective cause. Unfortunately, and regardless of background, many Airmen and Guardians join the military service with a low level of self-esteem. The reasons vary from previous traumatic experiences to the shock of leaving home and venturing upon the unknown to being challenged mentally and physically in ways they had never imagined.

Regardless of the circumstances, it is the job of NCOs to create the conditions that foster self-esteem and nurture self-worth in their teammates. If this is not done, you will get "a version" of your Airmen and Guardians at work, but it will not be the "best version" of them. NCOs have to give their subordinates room to grow, opportunities to experience higher levels of responsibility, leeway to fail, support to pick them back up, and reassurance along the way.

Verbal confirmations such as, "You did really well today," and "We couldn't have gotten it done without you" can go a long way to helping our coworkers embrace their self-worth. And when their performance does not meet expectations, constructive criticism such as, "You missed the target on that one, but I'm going to help you get it right," can have a very positive impact when you know your subordinates may be near a breaking point.

Our teammates must understand that while serving in the military is one the most honorable and exciting things a person can do, it does not define us as human beings. It is a part of us but not all of us. It is what we do, but not who we are at our essence. Who we are allows us to serve with selflessness, sacrifice, and commitment, not the other way around. One day, after four years or 30 years of service, the uniform has to come off permanently, and our self-worth should not come off with it. Upon separation or retirement, the goal is for every service member to walk away mentally, spiritually, physically, and emotionally healthy. Just as important is our teammates' overall health and self-esteem while serving on active duty or in the guard and reserves. NCOs should have the situational awareness to identify and the courage to engage when their fellow service-members are suffering from a lack of self-worth. Knowing what to say, when to say it and how to say it takes emotional intelligence.

**Emotional INTELLIGENCE (EI):** Emotionally Intelligent leaders know how their actions and words affect others. They also recognize changes in their followers' behaviors, attitudes, non-verbal communication cues, and response patterns. And they care. That is a crucial component of EI: caring. It does no good to recognize emotional indicators if you maintain indifference toward them.

Leaders who possess a productive level of EI are also self-aware. We all have prejudices and biases, and they creep into our decision-making processes from time to time. We sometimes create homogenous teams within our work centers, unconsciously exercising favoritism based on those biases. Have you seen an NCO who spends an excessive amount of time with female Airmen at the expense of mentoring male Airmen or hangs out with the other Guardians who share a similar interest in sports or cigars while excluding those teammates who do not? These favoritism actions are often unintentional but can rapidly degrade trust as those teammates on the short end of the stick feel that they are missing out on information, mentorship, and growth opportunities. Optics are important, and perception is reality to many.

NCOs who are interested in developing their EI must also work on growing their empathy for others. Empathy, in a nutshell, means putting oneself in the shoes of someone else. In light of everything that has occurred in American society over the last several years, consider these scenarios of an NCO struggling to connect with his Airman and honestly think about whether their differences are barriers to their professional relationship. Ask yourself how you would overcome these perceived barriers if you were the NCO mentioned. (1) It is well known that the NCO is a Republican, and his Airman is a Democrat. (2) The NCO is a devout Christian and youth minister, while his Airman is a Muslim. (3) The NCO grew up with both parents in the suburbs while his Airman grew up with a single parent in an impoverished neighborhood. (4) The NCO is against same-sex marriages, and his Airman is an outspoken member of the LGBT community. (5) The NCO shows up to an unofficial function with a "Build Back Better" hat on, and his Airman arrives with a "Make America Great Again" t-shirt. (6) The NCO encourages his teammates to attend base-sponsored cultural heritage, and diversity and inclusion (D&I) events. At the same time, his Airman voices his opinion that the military wastes too much time on D&I.

Any of the scenarios mentioned above can be reversed as far as a random NCO's personal positions and the unique positions of his Airmen. They may be extreme, but they are realistic. The real question is, how would you mend fences and build your professional relationship with your subordinate in the given scenarios? I can tell you this, it takes emotional intelligence and empathy. EI will allow you to lead as an NCO from a neutral position, and empathy will help you be receptive to hearing other viewpoints while trying to understand your subordinate's worldviews. You do not have to agree with different worldviews. Still, you do have to lead in such a way that your efforts and actions foster a trusting relationship that creates a culture of inclusion. And believe me, your Airmen and Guardians will know if you are not sincere. They are also always listening, so be careful and mindful of what you say regarding race, religion, politics, sexual orientation, etc. Build trust, develop your team and ensure everyone knows that they are necessary to the mission.

**NECESSARY to the Mission:** Everyone wants to feel like they matter. There are few things professionally worse than coming to work and doing a job that you believe does not matter. While serving as Command Chief for the 30th Space Wing at Vandenberg Air Force Base, California, the motto of our medical group immediately caught my attention. Their slogan was "We Launch Rockets!" Launching rockets and testing missiles was one of the primary purposes for the existence of our wing. The medical group commander wanted to ensure that every doctor, nurse, medical technician, dietician, immunization specialist, physical therapist, and bio-technician understood that what they did daily directly influenced the installation's ability to launch rockets. Each Airman was able to come to work every day with a sense of purpose. The mission could not get done unless the Airmen assigned to launch rockets and test missiles were healthy enough to do so.

Airmen and Guardians need to know that they are necessary to the mission... individually and collectively essential to the mission. NCOs must ensure that their subordinates know that they matter. What they do professionally counts, regardless of duty title, rank, or career specialty. Knowing that your team relies on you for mission accomplishment helps build a sense of pride and ownership in the tasks at hand. When a person knows that she matters, she tends to go the extra mile, do more than what is asked, and surpass what is expected.

It is an NCO's job to draw the link for Airmen between what they do daily and how it ties into the bigger mission. This means that NCOs should know the history of their bases and the missions affiliated with them. Whenever possible, they should get their Airmen out of their office spaces and onto the flight-line, etc., where their teammates can see the bigger mission up close and personal. NCOs must know how to W.I.N. to ensure we continue to produce the best Airmen, Guardians, enlisted warriors, and leaders the world has ever known!

# CHAPTER 10
## Q&A with Air and Space Chiefs!

* CMSgt April Brittain (US Space Force) – Senior Enlisted Leader, Space Delta 2, Peterson Space Force Base, CO.
* CMSgt Casy Boomershine – Command Chief, 502 ABW, JBSA, TX.
* CMSgt Karen "Liz" Cloyd – Command Chief, 388 FW, Hill AFB, UT.
* CMSgt Omar Basnight (US Space Force) – Senior Enlisted Leader, Space Launch Delta 45, Patrick Space Force Base, FL.
* CMSgt Ray Riley – Command Chief, 75 ABW, Hill AFB, UT.
* CMSgt Teresita Kobilis (AF Reserves) – Air Force Reserves Advisor, Barnes Center for Enlisted Education, AL.

**(Questions are answered in a conversational tone)**

## *As a Chief, what are your basic expectations for NCOs?*

**Chief Brittain:** The NCO tier is where you should really start to gain a deeper understanding of servant leadership, and you typically do that through involvement with your subordinates, authenticity, and transparency while never losing respect for others. This is really where you start to see leadership unfold. I expect that they are part of the solution versus part of the problem and that they'll be a bit bolder in using their voice to fix/shape the culture around them. I also expect them to begin to learn how to lead in their own way, as their true selves, versus mimicking others and trying to fit into some mold.

**Chief Boomershine:** Know your Airmen, and be involved in their lives and in their development. Care about the people in your charge, care about your fellow Airmen, and make sure that they know that you care. Understand that it's not about you or what you get. It's about what you have to give. Do your best to take care of people as they would like to be cared for. Be credible, and live by the core values and expectations defined in The Enlisted Force Structure, AFI 36-2618 and 1-1.

**Chief Cloyd:** Unfortunately, it's experience that teaches us what we really need from our NCOs. Basic expectations include: compassion – there is nothing that can't be worked through with compassion for what our fellow Airmen are dealing with. It's important to understand what we as individuals perceive as a minor situation, another person may view as a traumatic experience. Empathy – if we have empathy, we are more likely to listen to understand instead of to respond. Transparency – share missteps and lessons learned so that your team knows that you have had your own challenges that led you to grow.

**Chief Basnight:** One of the first things that I expect our NCOs to do is be transparent. We need to tell our folks the truth. NCOs need to provide candid feedback. Be honest, sincere, and act like you give a damn!!! This will help our folks improve, and I feel there is a high probability of a positive return in that investment from a real conversation. We need our NCOs to take pride in what they do!!!

Many of our folks are just going through the motions. I remember back in the day when we had to iron our uniforms and shine our boots. For me, this set the stage for taking pride in what you did. I could walk around and point out most folks who absolutely loved what they did because they looked sharp. It can be challenging to do that these days. NCOs need to know and understand what their personnel are doing each day.

NCOs have a responsibility to know their personnel on a professional level and to understand their personal challenges. Our NCOs must understand that they represent more than just themselves. NCOs must fulfill their responsibilities as an NCO, and this comes with demonstrating the whole person concept each and every day through action, not just words!!!

**Chief Riley:** Honestly, I start with the "little brown book." It tells you all the basics, and then I build on from there. My expectations are split between an NCO continuing to grow their leadership skills while mastering their AFSC. My expectations grow even more if an NCO has the privilege to serve as a supervisor. I won't lie; my expectations are great because an NCO has to take their supervisor's direction and execute on a daily basis. This is in addition to learning the demands of the job and learning and understanding what it takes to be an Airman in today's Air Force. Beyond the "little brown book," I expect an NCO to be a leader and even better follower. I expect them to be a motivator and have a sense of emotional intelligence beyond that of their peers who are not serving in the armed forces. I expect them to be driven and self-motivated, not at a robotic level… but that of someone who hopes and aims to be a little bit better tomorrow than they are today.

**Chief Kobilis:** My basic expectations are for NCOs to be technically proficient. An NCO should be well versed in their AFSC and have tactical expertise.

***How is being an NCO now different from being an NCO in the early 2000s?***

**Chief Brittain:** I think we honestly put more weight on their shoulders these days due to all of the downsizing and resource restraints we've been under for quite some time now. There are far fewer of them than there were of us, so that comes with greater responsibility. Though, I also feel like they have advantages as well. We equip them with life skills such as resiliency, mindfulness, emotional intelligence, etc., that the world has realized are essential soft skills they need to be a successful leader. They also reach E-5 much quicker than my generation, so most don't have as much road in their rearview. Their experience and exposure levels are not the same, which can make being an NCO more challenging for them. However, they don't shy away from a challenge and are definitely more willing to question why things are done a certain way. So, I honestly feel the NCOs of today will propel us further and faster than we did in the early 2000s.

**Chief Boomershine:** We are in a digital age, and it has revolutionized the way we learn and absorb data. Smartphones and social media have changed the way people communicate. In some ways, it's easier to communicate with your troops, and in other ways, it's gotten harder. One thing that remains the same is if you know your people, you'll learn how to reach them.

**Chief Cloyd:** We expect more of our Airmen as a whole today than we did before. There was a larger force in 2000, and taking care of others was a "nice" thing. We expected supervisors to do the right things for their Airmen, but intrusive leadership and mentorship weren't really something we talked about. If you were lucky, you had a supervisor who did those things naturally... but that kind of leadership wasn't expected.

In the early 2000s, there was a significant number of senior airmen getting promoted to staff sergeant [SSgt] (aka "The Great Staff Giveaway"). It seemed that there were so many SSgts that you could not throw a stick without hitting one! What happens when 3-5 years of promotion to SSgt was between 60-75%? There are more SSgts than junior Airmen.

Clearly, that means there were fewer Airmen assigned to a SSgt. A SSgt could be an average supervisor, and it may not be that noticeable. An NCO was not strained with taking care of more than one or two Airmen if they supervised one at all. Some career fields are so much smaller than others that it was common for an NCO to not have supervised anyone for several years. This lack of experience led to SNCOs who were less prepared than their predecessors.

**Chief Basnight:** Expectations are higher now, in my opinion. Our personnel are getting promoted a lot faster than I did in the 1990s and early 2000s. Our NCOs must professionally develop at a more rapid pace due to the increased amount of responsibility that has been levied on them due to the USAF downsizing. We also expect our NCOs to be educated. I'm not saying that our personnel were not smart way back when, but now they are expected to educate themselves at a younger age or get left behind.

**Chief Riley:** The first thing that I think of is that NCOs weren't as connected to everyone and everything during that timeframe. Nor did we ask as many questions during that time. It may have just been me, but as a staff sergeant, I don't remember being as involved with what's going on in the grander scale of things as our NCOs are today. I can tell you for sure I couldn't just hop online and drop a "DM" [direct message] to any senior enlisted member in the Department of Defense and honestly expect a response. But now, our Airmen at the lowest level have a direct line to the most senior leaders in the Department of Defense, and it's a good thing. In that same tone, though, I feel like I was more connected with my NCO peers back then than some of our NCOs are connected with their peers today. I may be wrong. It may just be me...

**Chief Kobilis:** The evolution of technology. Our current environment allows our Airmen to be vocal/immediately provide thoughts, refute/debate misinformation, and assemble like-minded groups at record speed. Although social media was available in the early 2000s, the capability wasn't as readily at everyone's fingertips. Computers/devices that are mobile were not financially possible to most households. Airmen still had to use libraries or schools to retrieve/respond to topics. Sometimes this lessened capability allowed for more thought to occur instead of our gut reactions. While I appreciate being responsive and instantaneously providing input to a matter, a delay in pondering critical components assists in empathy.

## *What is the biggest mistake you've seen NCOs make?*

**Chief Brittain:** Losing humility and gaining a chip on their shoulder. There's a lot of pride in putting on that first NCO rocker, but some quickly forget where they came from, which causes walls to go up between them and their subordinates. I've seen far too many try to use "rock, paper, stripes" as their way to influence a decision; stripes always win. This "chip" often comes out in lines such as, "It's called leadership, not likership" or "It's not personal, it's business." To me, those lines are copouts. It's better if your team likes and respects you; you're more cohesive and effective that way. And what may be a business decision to you often feels very personal to them. So, I think we need to better meet folks where they are and have more honest and helpful conversations to most effectively manage relationships. Just because you have a higher rank and can be a jerk doesn't mean you should be one.

**Chief Boomershine:** Giving away their authority. Often an NCO can help solve problems for their Airmen, but they are too quick to push that on to someone else rather than to attempt to solve the problem. I have seen many NCOs come to my office when I was a first sergeant, ready to drop off an Airman with a problem they could have solved. All that does is tell the Airman that you can't help them. If you can't help them get their pay straightened out, how on earth will they trust you to help when they are struggling with a significant personal issue? Your troops should know that you care, they can trust you, and you are there to help them.

**Chief Cloyd:** Often, the fear of making a mistake hinders NCOs. There is so much pressure to get it right that two things tend to happen. First, NCOs (and even SNCOs) will "contract their leadership" to another person. For example, when an Airmen approaches their supervisor with a problem, it is not surprising when their immediate response is, "Let's go ask the first sergeant or flight chief." While that is not a wrong answer, I wonder how much of that is driven by fear of making the wrong decisions? Second, NCOs will sometimes take what they have learned to be the absolute answer. Often, they assume that what they were told in the past is the correct answer and do not research to ensure the information is accurate or has not been updated.

**Chief Basnight:** Being selfish. I've seen quite a few NCOs that have grown to be more concerned about themselves than their subordinates. This has led them to focus on getting promoted or advancing to that next job at the expense of their wingman. To be honest, I don't blame them. This is the culture that we have created!! Our NCOs are in search of the blueprint for success. Often this leads them down the road of following a checklist, and when that formula doesn't work, they take it out on their subordinates. Which in turn leads to a lack of development amongst our younger folks.

**Chief Riley:** My mind starts to wander on this question. It would be easy to say getting a DUI, having inappropriate relationships with other Airmen, or using illegal substances (e.g., committing crimes). That said, the worst thing that I've seen is an NCO in a trusted leadership/supervision position truly... honestly... not care about the Airmen they are charged to lead. Hands down, this is probably the worst thing I've seen in a handful of our NCOs today. Airman: "I didn't get promoted this time around... Oh well." The Airman comes to an NCO: "Hey Sir/Ma'am, what can I do to increase my chances of getting promoted my next time out?" The NCO's answer: "Nothing. Don't even try... or just make sure you brown nose the superintendent, first sergeant, chief, and the commander; then your promotion is guaranteed!"

I believe an NCO in a leadership position who basically comes in to get paid, and nothing more, can be one of the most devastating obstacles an Airmen could ever be challenged by. Ask yourself this... who has a more significant effect on your day-to-day life as an Airman? Is it your squadron commander, or is it your immediate supervisor? Imagine an Airman led by an NCO for 3 years who could care less about them or anything that would help them become a better Airman.

**Chief Kobilis:** Rushing to make the next rank and forgetting that we are each other's wingmen. I have seen some NCOs move too quickly to be promoted to the next position/stripe and miss out on development where they currently are.

## What do you wish you would've known when you were an NCO?

**Chief Brittain:** I wish I would have known that you can land in a place of great happiness and success without creating unhealthy competition amongst your peers as you all fight to climb the corporate ladder. I wish I better knew and BELIEVED that keeping my head low, taking care of those entrusted to me, working hard, and trusting the system would be enough. Too often, we lose sight of that and weaken our overall military strength by trying to "one-up" each other to have a greater shot at getting a stratification, better job opportunity, etc. I wish I would have seen more NCOs and SNCOs lifting each other up versus seeing each other as rivals and tearing each other down.

**Chief Boomershine:** I wish I had known that it's okay not to have all the answers, and it's okay to ask for help. It's a gift to allow others to help you. Helping people feels good, so don't take that opportunity away from others because you let your ego get in the way of receiving help when you need it.

**Chief Cloyd:** Learn to work in the "gray." As an NCO, you have the ability to make decisions and take care of your people. If you understand the layers of each of your Airmen, you can make an impact by taking care of them and allowing them to fail forward while giving them room to grow and make mistakes. And not every mistake deserves paperwork. Start by talking to your Airmen. This will eliminate more confusion, frustration, and misunderstanding. If you think you are right, you may not be, and you should ask questions.

**Chief Basnight:** I wish I understood the importance of balancing my professional and personal development. I spent a lot of time driving towards being successful at my job. And I was very good at what I did at the time. What I didn't do is open my mind to the other educational opportunities that were placed before me. I had a significant lack of expanding my horizons outside of my professional career. I believe that this has impacted me to this day. Planning for the future must be a priority at a younger age. This comes with balancing work and your personal life.

**Chief Riley:** Honestly, I wish I was a little bit more resilient. As an NCO, I went through a pretty rough point in my life, and if it weren't for my friends that I was surrounded by during that time, I for sure would not be where I am today.

But I was lucky. I was surrounded by great people, at least my close circle. But a lot of Airmen today don't have that. They don't have that close circle. I wish I knew some of the tools and techniques that are taught and learned today regarding resilience. I wish I would have known that I could honestly go to mental health and have a good frank conversation about several things that were bothering me, and not be afraid of what someone may have thought or what may or may not have happened with the current job that I had; or my security clearance.

**Chief Kobilis:** I wish I had known exactly how many developmental opportunities were available throughout the wing. As a reservist, I believed that I had to stay within my squadron activities to receive good mentorship, provide mentorship, join groups, and interact with active duty (host base) programs. The separatism mentality began early in my career (ARC vs. RegAF) and caused me to delay involvement with base activities.

## How can NCOs best juggle family life and work-life?

**Chief Brittain:** You often hear leaders say, "You need to find balance." That doesn't resonate with me. I tell folks they need to "create balance." Balance isn't a Pokemon that you're going to magically stumble into and find. You need to create it, and you do that by putting yourself on your calendar and being pretty unapologetic about it. Too often, we see our calendar's white space as time for everyyyyyone else, but you need to block out time for yourself as well...to make the doctor's appointments you've been putting off for months, to go to your kid's soccer game, to take the one you love to lunch, etc. Block...It...Off....and hold yourself accountable to not dismiss your own reminders.

**Chief Boomershine:** Understand your priorities for both work and home life and what things refill your energy. Sometimes you will have tasks that you cannot drop at work, and sometimes you'll have tasks you can't drop at home. Know which ones are which, and understand less critical tasks will sometimes have to drop. Sometimes it will be work, and sometimes it will be family life. Protect your non-negotiable priorities, and do your best to not drop those. Ensure those things in your life that give you energy are built into your day and protect that as a non-negotiable.

**Chief Cloyd:** Communicate – talk to your family about what is going on at work (inspection preparation, upcoming deployments, programs that require additional attention).
Share with them why you are working longer hours, the stress you are under, and expectations. When your family understands why you are not at home, they are given a chance to support you with all of the information that you provide them.

Make them part of the team – your family should see where you work, know the people you work with, etc. If there is a squadron event, include them. Bring your significant other and your children to the unit when families are invited to attend. This gives them an idea of who you are working with, where you work and includes them in what happens in your life.

Go home on time – we know what time to come to work. We know what time lunch is (typically)… go home on time. Don't stay at work just because you can. There will always be work to do. There will always be emails to answer. The thing we need to remember is what things need immediate attention and what can wait until later.

Express when you need to take family time – you will never get back the time missed. Your kids need to see you at their soccer games and spending time with them doing homework. Your significant other needs to know you appreciate them and what they do. Make time for them. Tell your supervisor what you would like to do and share how important leaving an hour early, occasionally, can help you connect with your family. This will help when you can't be home and when there are long hours at work (or TDYs, deployments, etc.).

**Chief Basnight:** I'll start out by saying that I spent the first fifteen years of my career making work, and work only, my life. Family was secondary, and I'll be straight with you. I spent many years being a professional at work and a deadbeat dad at home. That was all on me!!! I didn't understand that you had to put in work and time to make family life work. I learned a lot from my younger days. I would advise all NCOs and our younger folks to ensure that your family is a part of your job. Explore options to bring them in to allow them to understand what you do. Make them understand how they are a significant part of your success. Celebrate them at your promotion ceremonies!!! Seems simple, doesn't it? I've run across many MSgts that have never had their family at a promotion ceremony and families that had no idea what their spouses did each day.

Make it a priority to be present at significant family events. Find ways to incorporate family life into work. And take LEAVE!!!!

**Chief Riley:** I have heard many different sayings from some of our most senior leaders on this very topic. I remember being told something about a 60, 20, 10 rule, or you should try and find balance, or work hard/play hard... whatever the hell does any of that even mean. What I know is that I work hard and I do my best to try and keep my wife informed of everything that's going on. I try to include her on as many Air Force-type things as I can (e.g., ALS graduations, picnics, other base events) and make an event out of it. I also try to keep as much peace in my household as possible. When I get off from work, I don't bring it home... That laptop stays at work and I try my best to not look at my work phone, or tackle emails while I'm spending quality time with my family.

The latest thing I'm hearing is trying to have a sense of harmony with work and family. I don't know if I have harmony, but I know how to read my wife and my family. I know when I'm spending too much time away from them and plugged into work. When it gets close to that point, I let go and ensure they get my time.

I have promised my wife that I will never miss anything important for my kids or her due to any common work meeting or reoccurring event. If there is a staff meeting and my kid made the honor roll, I'm going to go see her get her certificate. If my wife has a medical appointment and she wants me to be there, and I have an office visit, I'll be there next to my wife and will reschedule that office visit.

For me, harmony in this sense means there will sometimes be occasions where I give a little bit more to work and a little bit less of the day to my family. You must know when you get close to that tipping point on the scale. Then you push it slightly in the other direction giving more to your family and cutting back on some things from work... like extra hours and things of that nature.

Many won't agree, and many have been doing this their whole career and have awesome relationships with their family. You have to find what works for you; this dynamic may change if your spouse is military also. The most important thing is, find what works for you and your family. I have seen too many people go hard for the military to get that next job or that next promotion, only to be standing alone during their retirement ceremony... I pray that won't be me, and I pray that won't be you. Find... what... works...

**Chief Kobilis:** While our mission to serve is honorable and important, learning to prioritize family needs is necessary. Each family dynamic is unique. We must strive to find what levels of each are required. It is a constant evaluation of family events to mission requirements. The work-life is an obligation (pays our bills, provides healthcare, supports the enterprise), but family life is a responsibility (nourishes the soul, provides support in the form of our relatives/spouses, and provides love that is foundational).

### What is the NCO's role in Diversity & Inclusion?

**Chief Brittain:** Diversity is natural if you get inclusion right. We should never be exclusive, and if you find yourself in a room or friend circle with folks that only look and think like you, you're doing it wrong. There's so much greatness in the diversity of thought that gets lost because we too quickly shut down another's point of view and exclude them the moment we don't see eye to eye. When it comes to inclusion, do your part in making sure no one feels like an outsider or left behind...anything less does yourself and our service a huge injustice. Get out of your own head and spend time investing in one another. You'll be surprised at how many beautiful moments, valid points of view, and deeper connections exist that you are missing out on.

**Chief Boomershine:** People should feel that they belong and that the Air Force is their family. An NCO's role is to help establish that culture and connection. Diversity and inclusion are a natural part of that. NCOs must create a workplace that is inclusive and where people can see themselves reflected in leadership roles.

**Chief Cloyd:** Listen – everyone's experiences have led them to see the world in a certain way. Listen to their stories. Ask questions. Empathize. A person's experiences are what lead them to respond a certain way. Their reactions are not wrong. We have to understand that their feelings are important. Because people have these experiences, there is a natural response. This is not to say their reaction is always the best, but it is theirs. This happens because of the hormonal response associated with "fight, flight, or freeze." This biological change causes us to respond in a way that may not be clear to others. Help bridge gaps – when we take the time to get to know others, we are connecting. Ask meaningful questions that encourage conversations beyond the surface level. Discover the layers that make up those in your work centers. There will be so many things that surprise you.

Don't be cliquish – all too often, we gravitate to those who are similar to us. As a female, I could naturally gravitate towards other females. As a Chief, I could feel more at ease around other Chiefs. As a Texan... you get it. But here's the thing... the best thing I ever did was reach outside of my comfort zone. Joining the Air Force allowed me to get to know others who are different from me... and I am so grateful. Before I joined the Air Force, I had never experienced such diversity. Because of the Air Force, I have met people from all corners of the earth. What did that do for me? I grew to better understand differences of thought. I grew from having conversations where the opinions differed from mine. Because I invested time to know others from different walks of life, I can listen to and work for more inclusive things for all of our Airmen and their families. While many may be similar, no Airmen or two families are the same. You will find the most amazing people, and they will bring value to your life, and in turn, you will be able to better care for others.

As an NCO, you are charged with caring for those around you at the end of the day. You're responsible for taking care of any Airman you come in contact with, not just the ones you supervise. If you have biases that get in the way of that, you fail to meet that charge. Reach out to understand, listen, ask questions, and ensure you represent all Airmen.

**Chief Riley:** Our NCOs should be the standard-bearers for diversity and inclusion. These members are closer to the action at every level. They can see changes that can affect diversity and inclusion before almost anyone else. They need to know what diversity and inclusion truly mean, how they are affected, and what they particularly bring to this dynamic. They need not be afraid to ask certain questions and fear what someone may think of them when they're trying to better understand the dynamics at play in their particular unit when it comes to diversity and inclusion. Our NCOs, who are typically our first-line supervisors, have so much power in this area. I truly hope they understand this. It makes me proud to see a low level of tolerance in NCOs when it comes to those who may push back against diversity and inclusion, and be at such a level where they're just not putting up with any type of discrimination. Of course, these things still happen in our nation and even in our military at times. That said, the things I observed and even put up with when I was an SSgt, our NCOs today would squash the very moment those incidents happened. And that, my friend, makes me damn proud!

**Chief Kobilis:** NCOs must be aware of diversity and inclusion. We should ensure we have diversity of cultures, experiences, race, thoughts and perspectives. Our diversity should levy inclusion. If we include a diverse population, we learn and develop into better humans. Deliberate exposure to variety in any situation can enhance discussion, ideas, and critical thoughts.

## *What inspires you most about today's NCOs?*

**Chief Brittain:** I'm really impressed by their acceptance of and care for others. There's no greater time than now, I think, when Airmen and Guardians have had more opportunity to be their true authentic selves and be accepted. Our NCOs have led the way in teaching us all the importance of that. They demonstrate so much consideration and genuine concern in not suppressing another human being based on race, gender affiliation, sex, religion, etc. That has been nothing short of inspiring. I'm so proud of them for being so willing to use their voices to make a difference in everything, from the policies we draft to the dress and appearance standards we implement.

**Chief Boomershine:** Today's NCOs are incredibly curious, smart, and innovative, as well as better educated than ever before. They are thirsty for knowledge and ask questions that previous generations may not have thought to ask.

**Chief Cloyd:** Gosh, where do I begin? There are so many things I could mention that inspire me. At a foundational level, I am inspired by the heart of today's NCOs. They seem to understand that they are truly the one percent of American society. Specifically, today's NCO is focused on being a professional. They represent the best our country has to offer. Today's NCOs understand that they are the reason the Air Force is a strong powerhouse. And with that, today's NCOs demand more from their leaders. They expect the best from leaders, but we have to earn it. We have to earn their respect. It doesn't come merely because of the positions leaders have. Today's NCOs push those in leadership positions to be transparent. They ask questions both about professional and personal things. In a short answer... they expect honesty from us, and they deserve it. They are not afraid to speak their minds and use their voices.

Today's NCOs are smart! From academics to boots-on-the-ground intelligence, we have the most dynamic force. They are innovative. They find ways to make a difference. They have a drive that is beyond what I knew as an NCO. They push the envelope on executing the mission, and their pride exceeds the furthest stars.

Today's NCOs inspire me because no matter what the challenges are, they push forward. I cannot thank them enough for pushing me to continue to learn and grow. Being around them gives me so much hope and excitement for our future. I want to be the best person and leader for them. They deserve my best.

**Chief Basnight:** The NCOs of today are so smart. It just amazes me each day to walk around and see how educated our force is. Many of our personnel have degrees which is a stark change from when I entered the military in the early '90s. We need our personnel to be innovative, and I feel they have the expertise to lead us in that direction. As we make the push to a fully digital force, these NCOs are definitely postured to lead the charge!!!

**Chief Riley:** Just as we have a handful of individuals who should not be NCOs, we have a multitude more that are some of the greatest leaders our Department of Defense has ever seen. I personally believe that I have met the next four Chief Master Sergeants of the Air Force. We have some NCOs out there that always go the extra mile, that care more about their Airmen than themselves, and would literally give you the shirt off their back if it would make your day brighter. These men and women are emotionally intelligent, empathetic, and have a sense of belonging to something greater than themselves from probably the moment that they were born. So, to sum it up, what inspires me the most about today's NCOs? As great as some of our leaders are today, I can only imagine how great our future leaders will be tomorrow based on the skills they are learning and their talents today!

**Chief Kobilis:** Our Airmen have the ideas and enthusiasm to affect change. They are no longer required to sit quietly in the corner. We expect their thoughts to be brought to the table. We have opened the doors to autonomy for a NEW course of action. We encourage designs and proposals that the previous leaders did not have exposure to. Innovative!

***What should our NCOs be focused on for the future in the era of Great Power Competition/Strategic Competition?***

**Chief Brittain:** The Great Power Competition is the primary national security focus of the United States, and I think every NCO needs to understand how their job/role fits into the bigger picture and the capabilities that we bring to bear. Every one of us needs to understand who our adversaries are, their intent, and find ways to outpace them by continuously looking for opportunities to innovate and advance our overall readiness and warfighting postures. It's an all-domain fight at this point. China and Russia would love nothing more than to interrupt our democratic norms and American freedoms. Hence, it's important that every one of us seek ways to keep our competitive edge.

**Chief Boomershine:** Learn what we are facing, and understand the role they play in defense of our nation. Educate yourself on the National Defense Strategy, AF Doctrine 1-1, and read as much and as widely as you can from our senior leaders' reading lists. If you have the opportunity to sit in on a strategy brief or an intelligence brief, take it. Look for ways to do things better, more efficiently, or cheaper, and don't accept the status quo.

**Chief Cloyd:** Learn – Be the best at your job as a technician. We need you to focus on what needs to be done to learn everything possible in your job and to teach others. Don't be too proud to teach or share knowledge and information. The competition isn't your fellow NCOs. There is no time for, "I have a secret." Learn. Teach. Grow. Repeat.

Trust your Airmen – Give them time and space to fail forward. The competition isn't "us vs. them." You were once someone's headache... you are where you stand because of them. You need to give grace, time, and have patience.

Listen to what your senior leaders say – From the National Defense Strategy to what's happening in the world, know what's going on around us. Figure out how we fit in. Your Airmen have questions, and you are where they are looking for answers. You don't have to have all of the answers. Just be ready to connect them to what our country asks of its Airmen.

**Chief Basnight:** From a US Space Force perspective, we are developing a culture of agility, innovation, and boldness. We need our Guardians to feel empowered to fail forward. Empowerment is one of the keys to our success for our nation. I believe that training and education are the foundation for empowering our personnel to be agile, innovative, and bold. During this era of Great Power Competition, training and education will have to be a focus for our NCOs now and in the future. Our nation's success depends on it!!!

**Chief Riley:** What can I do in my current job, at my current level, in my current grade… to accelerate change! What can I do to ensure that I am a living example of General Brown's Accelerate Change or Lose and a living demonstration of execution for his action orders? We have to live this. We have to understand where we fit in the bigger picture. We can't just look to the next assignment. We have to look at what the next 10, 20, 30, 40 years will look like… and then, you have to ask yourself, "What can I do today to make sure that Airmen 40 years from now are set up for success." And once you identify that, you have to get after it like your life depends on it. It's a lofty goal, but so was the United States Air Force itself…

**Chief Kobilis:** NCOs should stay informed. They should constantly seek out an understanding from differing credible sources and always think outside of the box. With the expansion of technology, contested platforms, and cyber/security threats, Airmen can assist in shaping the environment and improvement of our strategic objectives.

# CHAPTER 11

## Today's Threat, Tomorrow's War

NCOs must understand and explain to their subordinates that the Great Power Competition (GPC) is not just a buzzword. We are no longer fighting your father's war (Operation DESERT STORM) or your older brother's war (Operation ENDURING FREEDOM). Our strategies today must be different from what they were during your grandfather's war (Vietnam). We must be mentally and operationally prepared for the dire consequences of conventional conflicts involving nuclear powers that could produce casualties on the scale of your beloved great-grandfather's war (World War II). As former President Ronald Reagan stated,

> "Freedom is never more than one generation away from extinction. We didn't pass it to our children in the bloodstream. It must be fought for, protected, and handed on for them to do the same, or one day we will spend our sunset years telling our children and our children's children what it was once like in the United States where men were free." [1]

To remain informed on the latest news involving Strategic Competition (formally referred to as the Great Power Competition), I highly encourage leaders to download a **credible** news application on their smartphone. Then save China, Russia, North Korea, and Iran (at a minimum) in their favorites on the app. Following **credible** news on Africa, India, Latin America, space exploration and advancements, emerging technologies, etc., is also an excellent way to stay engaged. Knowledge is power, and NCOs must find a way to stay informed and abreast of international issues. Spending just 15-30 minutes a day reading news on a **credible** app can significantly change or enhance your understanding of global issues. I stress the word **"credible"** as there is an overwhelming appetite among many people today to base decisions and opinions off of fake or extremely one-sided news often found on unofficial websites and within social media.

**Strategic Competition:** Is the Strategic Competition threat concern for service members? If you are serving on active duty or in the guard or reserves, you better believe it is! And Strategic Competitors, along with their militaries, are concerned about and studying you. A key component to their sought-after success is building a profile on the most envied enlisted corps in the world; that is you. What motivates you? What pisses you off? They are watching. What do you post on social media? How do you feel about your military leaders? The Strategic Competitors are studying you. What are your weaknesses as an enlisted corps? What are your vulnerabilities? How easy do you buy into false and fabricated social media posts, videos, and comments? They are taking notes. Do societal unrest and political strife in the US affect the readiness and focus of the enlisted corps? Can the love that American citizens have for their military be altered or shifted? Our enemies want to know.

The Strategic Competitors are important enough to have been a significant focus in our president's Interim National Security Strategic Guidance released in March 2021, the US Intelligence Community's Annual Threat Assessment released in April 2021, the Summary of the 2018 National Defense Strategy released by former SecDef Jim Mattis, the

Description of the National Defense Strategy 2018 released by the Joint Staff, and CSAF C.Q. Brown's strategy of Accelerate Change or Lose released in August 2020.[2] The point is that as NCOs, you need to pay attention and learn as much as you can about today's threat and tomorrow's war. Do not get caught sleeping on the job!

China plans to be the leading global economic, strategic and military power, displacing America's position by 2049 in alignment with the centennial of their Communist revolution.[3] Their Belt and Road Initiative, man-made islands, and their activities in the space domain are a critical part of that plan. Russia remains a significant nuclear threat,[4] continues to hold joint military drills with China,[5] and has taken great efforts to hack and interfere with US elections.[6]

North Korea continues to scoff at the US presence in South Korea while making threats and testing their ballistic missile capabilities as a show of force and aggression in the region.[7] They also exert a lot of energy into hacking global banks and institutions.[8] Iran continues to be a threat to the US and our forces in the Middle Eastern region, even under heavy sanctions. They shot down an American drone over the Strait of Hormuz in 2019, and the US has carried out airstrikes against Iran-backed militias.[9] The relationship continues to be one of tension which was heightened when the US pulled out of the "Iran Nuclear Deal." Our strategy for the ground wars and uncontested air attacks of the Global War on Terrorism has shifted to focusing on the potential "high-end" fight with our Strategic Competitors. The question is, are you ready?

Every generation of Americans has had a group of men and women to stand watch against those who would do us harm. When necessary, they took the fight forward, seeking out and destroying our adversaries where they slept. Those American men and women, those warriors, were like sheepdogs and wolfhounds. The sheepdogs stood watch, addressing and attacking any foe that presented itself in a threatening manner. The wolfhounds sought out their enemies, bringing total destruction to their evil sanctuaries when they found them. Every generation of Americans has had a group of men and women to stand watch. This is your generation, NCOs. This is your watch!

-------

Afghanistan: As I prepared to publish this book, the US military withdrawal from Afghanistan happened. "America's longest war" abruptly came to an end, and it caused varying emotional responses from both military and non-military citizens alike. Countless service members have served tours in that specific region of the world. They have invested a lot into our efforts to combat terrorism while bringing hope to the Afghan people. Some questioned whether our efforts were in vain. Many were confused about why we pulled out, while others were enraged at how our forces were pulled out.

Like you, several of my friends have both visible and invisible wounds from the war in Afghanistan. It also goes without saying that we must never forget that some gave all. Many of us missed birthdays, holidays, and special events during our time in Afghanistan. Still, some of our brothers and sisters gave their lives, literally. War is ugly, violent, and unforgiving. We are warriors, but we are thoughtful, caring, and compassionate. The world saw that in plain sight.

No US service member served in Afghanistan in vain. Let me repeat that. What we as US military members did in Afghanistan was…not…in…vain. Because of NCOs just like you, Americans have rested peacefully at night without concern for attack from foreign enemies. Afghan men, women, and children have been given opportunities for a better way of life, in countless cases, because of the actions and support of our military forces. We are the generation that responded to the tragic events of September 11, 2001. We are the generation that secured our homeland and brought some semblance of stability to an unstable global environment. Unfortunately, that does not free us from the burden of fighting to rationalize how 20 years of effort came to an abrupt end with chaos ensuing around departing aircraft. The images are burned into our memory. Personally, I do my best to focus on the thousands of souls on board those aircraft being airlifted by some of America's bravest heroes and aircrews. To the men and women involved in the evacuations and the rescues of countless other people in Afghanistan, I offer my heart-felt, "Thank you!"

Like many of my fellow veterans and NCOs, I was there …in Afghanistan. In 2011, following weeks of combat skills training, and just a month or two after my beautiful bride came to live with me, I led a six-person firefighting team from Joint Base Lewis-McCord in Washington State to a forward operating base in Kunduz, Afghanistan. We were a J.E.T. (Joint Expeditionary Tasking) team which means we were assigned to an army unit. An elite Blackhawk Medical Evacuation (medevac) detachment, to be exact. Upon arrival, we realized that our resources were scarce. We had two P-19 aircraft rescue firefighting vehicles and minimal equipment. To best utilize our staffing and provide decent downtime, I established a rotation. Two combat firefighters were positioned at our off-post airfield for 8 to 12 hours a day (outside-the-wire), two responded to the on-post helicopter pad for medevac emergencies, and two stood by, on-call for backup. I will not share the stories in this book, but I will confirm that serving in a combat environment can change a person.

Living on a forward operating base 288 miles from Bagram Airfield when Osama Bin Laden was killed and during the tenth anniversary of September 11, 2001, was interesting…and it changes you. Your daily interaction with the Afghan people changes you. The sound and vibrations of army tanks firing off rounds during times other than training change you. Seeing the US and coalition troops injured and killed…changes you. The selfless men and women who served in Afghanistan will never forget how that country changed them, much like the veterans who served in World War I & II, the Korean War, Vietnam, Operation DESERT STORM, and Operation IRAQI FREEDOM carried the memories of their service.

Now the question becomes, will we have to return? Will NCOs in your generation have to return? Will alliances be made between the Taliban and China or Russia? Will our global competitors seek a strategic advantage as a result of our military withdrawal? Will Afghanistan become a safe haven and breeding ground for terrorist groups? How do Afghanistan and the entire Middle East play into the strategic competition? And if we have to return…with extreme violence and prejudice…will you be ready? The answers to those rhetorical questions should be on the minds of every NCO in the profession of arms.

The one thing that I am sure of is that the US military has to be the one unwavering force when a crisis arises. NCOs have got to be ready, in uniform and out of uniform, at work and online. Online? Yes! Immediately after the Afghanistan withdrawal was announced, media outlets and various other groups sought to get reactions from service members and their families. Unfortunately, several took the bait. While responses and opinions in and of themselves are not wrong, all NCOs must be aware that one outburst, politically charged rant, or verbal attack on US leadership can degrade their chain of command, morale, and efforts made by thousands of service members. That is precisely why, when asked about my personal opinion on the withdrawal from Afghanistan, I gave the following response. I hope that it helps NCOs to remember our obligations and oath as service members.

### My social media post:

*"**The World**:* Chief, how do you feel about us pulling out of Afghanistan? Are you pissed? Should our troops be outraged?

*Me:* Every day that the good Lord blesses me to wake up and put on my Operational Camouflage Patten uniform, I'm thankful. I'm thankful for another day to serve our great nation. America isn't perfect but she's mine and I love her. I love her so much that I raised my hand and, in essence, agreed to give my life if required, so that she can continue to be brightened as the beacon of hope for the world. My oath didn't have stipulations. It didn't require that I agree with every decision and be consulted before every military action. My oath has meaning... a lot of meaning to me; meaning beyond the words that it entails. I refuse to question publicly or undermine the efforts of my chain of command or my military and civilian leadership. I refuse to be motivated by headlines that intentionally or unintentionally divide the cohesion of my brothers and sisters in arms.

I promise to lead the men and women in my care from a position of neutral, fairly with justice and empathy. My Airmen and Guardians have a voice. I will listen to them, especially when they are concerned or hurting. But I also accept my responsibility to help shape their perspectives, refocus their energies, and ensure that they never take their eyes off of the target. We are the sword and shield for our nation. We must not be swayed. If it were that asteroids darted towards the earth, institutions failed, and society lost hope for tomorrow…even on that apocalyptic day… Americans must know without a shadow of a doubt that the US military stands faithfully strong as the last best hope for our nation; ready when needed regardless of circumstance.

I have thoughts but they will not interfere with my duties. I have feelings but they will not be expressed in a way that plants any seeds of doubt among my teammates. I have opinions but they are not as important as what is best for the men and women standing guard at my right and left. I have freedoms but I have sacrificed many of them, temporarily, while I serve my nation as a warrior clothed in the uniform of our country. I am thankful that I have the blessed honor to stand guard…on the shoulders of giants and in the footsteps of the men and women who fought so hard before me while wearing our nation's cloth. How do I feel about Afghanistan? I'm on-call, as always. America has my number. I hope that answers your questions!"

[1] (n.d.). "Ronald Reagan – Quotes – Quotable Quotes." *Good Reads*.
[2] Air Force News Service (2020). "CSAF releases Action Orders to Accelerate Change Across Air Force." *US Air Force*.
[3] J. Mauldin (2019). "China's Grand Plan To Take Over The World.: *Forbes*.
[4] P. Geller & P. Brookes (2021). "The Increasing Russian Nuclear Threat." *The Heritage Foundation*.
[5] C. Deng (2021). "China, Russia Hold Military Drills Amid Security Concerns in Afghanistan, Central Asia." *The Wall Street Journal*.
[6] CNN Editorial Research (2020). "2016 Presidential Campaign Hacking Fast Facts." *CNN*.
[7] K. Tong-Hyung (2021). "N Korea repeats threat as US says joint drills are defensive." *AP*.
[8] E. Geller (2021). "North Korea hackers are 'the world's leading bank robbers,' U.S. charges." *Politico*.
[9] J. Walsh (2021). "Here's Why Tensions Are Rising Between Iran And The U.S." *Forbes*.

# CHAPTER 12
## The Last Best Hope for America

It has been a tumultuous few years in our nation, but the unfettered American spirit continues to shine through. I have heard that there are two Americas, and I agree, but not how you may imagine. I have learned that there is the America I see in the media, and there is the America that I experience every day. From time to time, it is a good idea to turn off your television, put down your cell phone and take a look at the men and women around you. Look at the diversity. Look at the professionalism. Look at the commitment to excellence and the innovative ideas. Look at the patriotism. Look at the smiles and laughter. Look at the sacrifices. Look at the charity. Look at the love. Look at the hope. When I look at my surroundings, I see Airmen, Guardians, and other service members and their families. I see the last best hope for America.

Spending too much time looking at the news media generally depresses me, while looking at my fellow service members tends to lift my spirit. So what do you spend your time looking at? To echo and paraphrase the sentiments of former US Secretary of State Colin Powell: "The [Air Force and Space Force] are living the domestic ideal ahead of the rest of America."

Air Force and Space Force bases are not just a microcosm of America; they are a microcosm of what America could be. Our communities are safe, diverse and every family is employed. There are activities for the youth, and base residents tend to get involved with special events and community celebrations. We breed healthy families, academic scholarship, and responsible citizenship. I am a huge believer that every off-base community that has service members living in it should be better because we are there. We are living and exuding the American dream.

There is a reason that most Americans still consider the US Military to be their most trusted public institution.[1] When politics become divisive, we hold the line. When society becomes outraged, we hold the line. When natural disasters strike, we hold the line. When a medical crisis hits, we hold the line. When war is imminent and American soil is threatened, we hold the line. When someone has to sacrifice their freedoms for the good of the country, we hold the line. And when America needs a beacon of hope to look to while visualizing what our nation could be, we proudly stand shoulder to shoulder, each service member in line!

The US Military is the A-team, the starting line-up. NCOs, this is YOUR team. Second place is not an option in our business. Our focus is not on product market research or shareholder versus stakeholder politics. On the best days, we bring peace and stability to the world. On the worst days, when a nation-state or terror group threatens our families and our way of life, we load up, launch and light up international skies like the 4th of July! We are both the aid you need during tragedies and the consequence you do not want to suffer during war. We will not falter, and we cannot fail. We are America's last best hope! **Hoorah, Air Force!!! Semper Supra!!!**

---

[1] C. Andrews (2019). "What public institution do Americans trust more than any other? Hint: It's not the media." *USA Today*.

# Bibliography

Air Force News Service (2020). "CSAF releases Action Orders to Accelerate Change Across Air Force." US Air Force. https://www.af.mil/News/Article-Display/Article/2442546/csaf-releases-action-orders-to-accelerate-change-across-air-force/

Andrews, Coleman (2019). "What public institution do Americans trust more than any other? Hint: It's not the media." USA Today. https://www.usatoday.com/story/money/2019/07/08/military-is-public-institution-americans-trust-most/39663793/

Braimah, Ayondale (2014). "John Hanks Alexander (1864-1894)." Black Past. https://www.blackpast.org/african-american-history/alexander-john-hanks-1864-1894/

Brown, C.Q. (2020). "Here's what I'm thinking about." Pacific Air Forces. https://www.pacaf.af.mil/News/Article-Display/Article/2210485/heres-what-im-thinking-about/

Carrega, Christina & Ghebremedhin, Sabina (2020). "Timeline: Inside the investigation of Breonna Taylor's killing and its aftermath." ABC News. https://abcnews.go.com/US/timeline-inside-investigation-breonna-taylors-killing-aftermath/story?id=71217247

Chappell, Bill (2021). "An All-Black Unit That Fought Germany And Racism In WWI Gets Congressional Gold Medal." https://www.npr.org/2021/08/31/1032821209/an-all-black-unit-that-fought-germany-and-racism-in-wwi-gets-congressional-gold-

CNN Editorial Research (2020). "2016 Presidential Campaign Hacking Fast Facts." CNN. https://www.cnn.com/2016/12/26/us/2016-presidential-campaign-hacking-fast-facts/index.html

Deng, Chaeo (2021). "China, Russia Hold Military Drills Amid Security Concerns in Afghanistan, Central Asia." The Wall Street Journal. https://www.wsj.com/articles/china-russia-hold-military-drills-amid-security-concerns-in-afghanistan-central-asia-11628692003

Dewberry, Joshua (2021). "Air Force unveils new mission statement." U.S. Air Force. https://www.af.mil/News/Article-Display/Article/2565837/air-force-unveils-new-mission-statement/#:~:text=The%20Air%20Force%20released%20its,airpower%20anytime%2C%20anywhere.&text=The%20ability%20to%20fight%20and,adversaries%2C%20according%20to%20service%20leaders

Editors of Encyclopedia Britannica (n.d.). "Three-fifths compromise." Brittanica. https://www.britannica.com/topic/three-fifths-compromise

Fargey, Kathleen (2014). "6888th Central Postal Directory Battalion. https://history.army.mil/html/topics/afam/6888thPBn/index.html

Friedman, Lindsay (2017). "10 Inspiring MLK Quotes on Leadership and Purpose." Entrepreneur. https://www.entrepreneur.com/article/269728

Garamone, Jim (2019). "Noncommissioned Officers Give Big Advantage to U.S. Military." U.S. Dept of Defense. https://www.defense.gov/Explore/News/Article/Article/2011393/noncommissioned-officers-give-big-advantage-to-us-military/

Geller, Eric (2021). "North Korea hackers are 'the world's leading bank robbers,' U.S. charges." Politico. https://www.politico.com/news/2021/02/17/us-charges-north-korean-hackers-wannacry-sony-469406

Geller, Patty-Jane & Brookes, Peter (2021). "The Increasing Russian Nuclear Threat." The Heritage Foundation. https://www.heritage.org/defense/report/the-increasing-russian-nuclear-threat

Haynes, Mareshah (2012). "Thomas N. Barnes: First African-American CMSAF." US Air Force. https://www.af.mil/News/Article-Display/Article/111618/thomas-n-barnes-first-african-american-cmsaf/

History.com Editors (2021). "Buffalo Soldiers." https://www.history.com/topics/westward-expansion/buffalo-soldiers

Ichimura, Anri (2020). Kobe Bryant, Basketball Icon and Venture Capitalist: 15 Quotes from Mamba on Success, Failure, and Work Ethic.: Esquire. https://www.esquiremag.ph/money/movers/kobe-bryant-quotes-a00304-20200129-lfrm2

Kabra, Hetal (2021). "Starbucks Net Worth 2021." MD Daily Record. https://mddailyrecord.com/starbucks-net-worth-2021-2022-2023

Mauldin, John (2019). "China's Grand Plan To Take Over The World.: Forbes. https://www.forbes.com/sites/johnmauldin/2019/11/12/chinas-grand-plan-to-take-over-the-world/?sh=7dbda03a5ab5

(n.d.). "12th Chairman of the Joint Chiefs of Staff: General Colin Luther Powell." Joint Chiefs of Staff. https://www.jcs.mil/About/The-Joint-Staff/Chairman/General-Colin-Luther-Powell/

(n.d.) "555th Parachute Infantry." http://triplenickle.com/history.htm

(n.d.). "Black Soldiers in the U.S. Military During the Civil War." National Archives. https://www.archives.gov/education/lessons/blacks-civil-war

(n.d.). "Colonel Charles Young." National Park Service. https://www.nps.gov/chyo/learn/historyculture/colonel-charles-young.htm

(n.d.). "Juneteenth: 'The Emancipation Proclamation – Freedom Realized and Delayed.'" Prairie View A&M Unviersity. https://www.pvamu.edu/tiphc/research-projects/juneteenth-the-emancipation-proclamation-freedom-realized-and-delayed/

(n.d.). "Lieutenant Henry Ossian Flipper: US Army, 1856-1940." Center of Military History. https://history.army.mil/html/topics/afam/flipper.html

(n.d.). "Me in a Nutshell." Merryl Tengesdal. https://merryltengesdal.com/

(n.d.). "Ronald Reagan – Quotes – Quotable Quotes." Good Reads. https://www.goodreads.com/quotes/13915-freedom-is-never-more-than-one-generation-away-from-extinction

(n.d.). "Say It Plain, Say It Loud: A Century of Great African American Speeches." American Radio Works. http://americanradioworks.publicradio.org/features/blackspeech/cpowell.html

(n.d.). "The Golden Thirteen." Naval History and Heritage Command. https://www.history.navy.mil/content/history/nhhc/browse-by-topic/diversity/african-americans/golden-thirteen.html

(n.d.). "The Tuskegee Airmen." Tuskegee University. https://www.tuskegee.edu/support-tu/tuskegee-airmen

(n.d.) "Thoughts On The Business Of Life." Forbes Quotes. https://www.forbes.com/quotes/11194/

O'Neal, Bylonnae (2020). "George Floyd's mother was not there, but he used her as a sacred invocation." National Geographic. https://www.nationalgeographic.com/history/article/george-floyds-mother-not-there-he-used-her-as-sacred-invocation

Sawchik, Travis (2021). "In The Age Of Velocity, Should MLB Teams Be Placing More Emphasis On Command?" Baseball America. https://www.baseballamerica.com/stories/in-the-age-of-velocity-should-mlb-teams-be-placing-more-emphasis-on-command/

SI Staff (2013). "The 10 Most powerful pitchers in baseball history." SI/MLB. https://www.si.com/mlb/2013/03/08/power-week-baseball-pitchers

The Inspector General Department of the Air Force (2020). "Report of Inquiry/Independent Racial Disparity Review." https://www.af.mil/Portals/1/documents/ig/IRDR.pdf

Tong-Hyung, Kim (2021). "N Korea repeats threat as US says joint drills are defensive." AP. https://apnews.com/article/health-coronavirus-pandemic-daf3e3bcb32414d531286039300d4cbe

Walsh, Joe (2021). "Here's Why Tensions Are Rising Between Iran And The U.S." Forbes. https://www.forbes.com/sites/joewalsh/2021/01/01/heres-why-tensions-are-rising-between-iran-and-the-us/?sh=5f8bf6ea4585

Zhang, Brenda (2021). "How Much Is Amazon Worth." Yahoo! Finance. https://finance.yahoo.com/news/much-amazon-worth-211405903.html?guccounter=1&guce_referrer=aHR0cHM6Ly93d3cuZ29vZ2xlLmNvbS8&guce_referrer_sig=AQAAAMp4Mdq93KWIMfNbmcmHx2eTZMTMQtgxmBaR4sS37FjK3j0Ka4glRx0QpNB1aHFuZ4oNaQtJc2rTE7iXREG54pGlho7CIFka3hto1o51FhSmHJOa4ufQIWBaQDNbbod4KCaLjGe0_foTxAWgjdeQXTWcN3-mr3CGpYH9IX__WkJe

DARYL J. HOGAN JR.

# Acknowledgments

"Thank you" to the men and women of the Air Force Sergeants Association (AFSA), especially AFSA's executive team. I have long wanted to write a book that would add value and perspective to the thousands of professional non-commissioned officers serving within our ranks. While attending the AFSA Conference in 2021, I was "re-blued," as they say, and inspired to write this book. Keep up the great work! I truly appreciate all that you do for Airmen, Guardians, and our families. Your impact and efforts transcend all of the branches of our beloved military.

"Thank you" to Chiefs April Brittain and Casy Boomershine (my Diamond sisters forever); Chiefs Ray Riley and Liz Cloyd (Hill AFB Airmen hit the lottery with you two); and Chiefs Omar Basnight and Tess Kobilis (two solid and compassionate leaders). One of the best parts of serving with the US Air Force and US Space Force was getting to serve with Chiefs (wingmen, leaders, warriors) like you. I think we made history with this one! You all are good friends, and your input and perspectives in this book will have an impact greater than you could ever imagine for years to come.

"Thank you" to Lt Col Nancy Clemens for reviewing this book and providing a vector check for me. When it comes to commissioned officers, you are one of the best and I appreciated your contributions and passion while serving as the 30th FSS Commander at Vandenberg AFB, California. Your wit and timely quips made otherwise boring weekly meetings fun and light-hearted. It must be the former enlisted Airman in you!

## About the Author

Daryl J. Hogan Jr. grew up in the Watts and Lynwood sections of Los Angeles County, California, before enlisting in the US Air Force in 1995. He has an extensive background in firefighting operations, having spent sixteen years in fire and emergency services, including four years as a fire instructor at the Louis F. Garland Department of Defense Fire Academy, before becoming a first sergeant in 2012.

Defying the odds, he rapidly progressed in his career and was promoted to the rank of chief master sergeant in 2017. In accomplishing that milestone, Daryl entered the top enlisted rank in the US Air Force held by only 1 percent of its enlisted members. Since his promotion, he has served as the Command First Sergeant for Air Force Space Command, the Command Chief Master Sergeant for Vandenberg Air Force Base during the establishment of the US Space Force, and as the Commandant for the Department of the Air Force's Chief Master Sergeant Leadership Academy, the pinnacle leadership experience for select enlisted members.

Over the course of a twenty-five-year career, Daryl has obtained five college degrees, including three Community College of the Air Force associate degrees, a bachelor's degree in fire science, and a master's degree in organizational leadership, both from Columbia Southern University. He has also been awarded several military honors, including the Legion of Merit, eight Meritorious Service Medals, and multiple First Sergeant of the Year awards. As of the publishing of this book, Daryl is pursuing his doctorate degree through Liberty University.

www.ingramcontent.com/pod-product-compliance
Lightning Source LLC
Chambersburg PA
CBHW052328220526
45472CB00001B/327